BETWEEN THE SHEETS

True Tales of a Woman's Pleasure at Sea

BY MADAME BUTTERFLY

This book is dedicated to all the men who made this story possible.

Table of Contents

Introduction

This is the true story of a woman who discovered a fascinating new way of living, refreshingly different to the rat race she had become trapped in. This new world was full of machoism, sexism and a complete lack of political correctness. Brizo entered a world where she was constantly surprised that being her filthy and inappropriate self was instantly accepted and even welcomed. She had glided into the world of sailing. The rough and rugged unkempt sailor types kept her dripping wet both in and out of the water. While Brizo was frustrated with the sexism that exists on deck, she was pleasantly surprised to discover that women are respected for taking charge on dick. She found herself in a world where women were given credit for having many lovers and for being assertive in the bedroom. I suppose when the ratio of men is so much higher than that of women, a sailor is grateful he's secured a mermaid on his hook.

SEBASTIAN

CHAPTER 1

Memories of the last two blissful and surreal years flashed before my eyes as the bus sped away with my forbidden beloved lover. Sebastian had his hand on the window of the bus with tears running down his face. The sight of this pathetic act of romance melted my heart. This was one reason why I loved him so much. Sebastian was my first Latino lover and his daily showers of affection and compliments made me feel like the most desirable woman alive. Despite the fact he was 17 years my senior, Sebastian's sexual appetite surpassed that of any younger lover I ever had. He was extremely talented in the art of sexual gratification and ensured I had orgasms daily no matter what the circumstance.

Like the time we were on charter and he whispered in my ear to grab a snorkel mask and meet him in the dinghy before any of the guests had a chance to ask what we were doing. I thought he was just giving me a break from the demands of the job, but it turns out that he couldn't resist the sight of my slender, toned, sun kissed feminine physique. As soon as we were out of sight, he stopped the engine and told me to lie down. He pulled my bikini to the side and dived for my precious pearl with that strong thick tongue of his. He was the most considerate lover I had to date, sending electric vibes of lust through my body as he explored every inch of me as if it were for the first time. After I was wet enough and moaning with intense pleasure, he untied my bikini bottom, pulled out his mast and penetrated me with deep passion The grip dots on the floor of the dinghy must've made for uncomfortable thrusting, but it didn't faze him as he whispered Spanish sweet nothings into my ear and repeated, "Que rico!" as he reached his ultimate pleasure. Yes, I would certainly miss that and the amazing sailing lifestyle we had.

Sebastian was my introduction into this new way of living. We were one of a fleet of sail boats that sailed backpackers between Panama and Colombia. It was a five day trip that most passengers thought was heaven. I on the other hand, thought it was five days of hell. The boat took on more passengers than there were beds, forcing us to leave our beautiful love nest in the bow to sleep on the hard slanted deck, dodging raindrops during the wet season. They invaded my home and disrespected our space. I had to fake a good mood in front of passengers, who never left a tip in appreciation and Sebastian exhausted himself trying to make me as happy and comfortable as possible.

The boat we worked on was the smallest in the fleet. Most of the backpackers wanted a party with lots of people, so we were the least busy of them all. It suited me just fine. In between charters, I was able to make the boat my home and spread out my belongings. As soon as we went below deck, we stripped ourselves of our clothes. The Caribbean heat was so intense that anything touching our sun kissed bodies would only cause more sweat. The sexual energy was so vibrant between us that revealing our tan lines made it easier to ravish each other's bodies the moment the urge passed through one of us. When we were on standby in Colombia, we often sailed two hours to a beautiful little bay no one ever visited. This allowed us to spend all of our time below and above deck disrobed. It was like our own little private lagoon. I used to love waking up naked in the morning and running off the back of the stern into the refreshing salty water. It's a better wakeup call than coffee. Whenever we finished a sweaty passionate love making session, clean up was easy. We giggled our way to the deck where we playfully jumped in to rinse away the remnants of our passionate desires.

Now that was all gone. We had spent the last two weeks in Miami to determine if Sebastian could live and work in the States. He quickly decided American culture was not for him and he wanted to return home to his beloved Colombia. The decision was sparked by a job offer to run another boat in Cartagena. That's where his heart was. That's where my heart was too, but when he asked me to go with him, I couldn't say yes. It wasn't just the heat of Cartagena and the near poverty living status we were barely surviving on. I had a taste of the sea and spent the last two years hearing wild stories of what sailors got up to all over the ocean. I wanted to climb more than just one mast and would do just that. As I watched the bus disappear into the distance with Sebastian's tears no doubt still rolling down, I had no idea of the scandalous sea adventures that were coming my way.

BENITO

CHAPTER 2

As I sat in the airport lounge, my mind played back to the last two incredible years of my life. A year after I started sailing with Sebastian, I searched for a boat to cross the Atlantic as I was already hearing stories of tanned, muscular, firm bodied younger sailors in Europe. I had a phone interview with a 64 year old Italian man named Fabio. During the phone interview, he seemed jovial and kind, so I agreed to fly to Jamaica where he and the boat were. I arrived one week before the other crew in order to prepare for the adventure. He had recently undergone heart surgery (red flag number 1), so he was unable to do everything himself. He sat at the saloon table smoking cigarette after cigarette zapping me of oxygen as he ordered me around. It was apparent throughout our week together, that he was not jovial and indeed was very angry and rude to others (red flag number 2). I started looking for an escape route as I knew sooner or later, the rudeness would turn in my direction.

I messaged Valerie and Robin, who were long time friends of Sebastian's. Earlier in the month, they had sailed from Colombia to Isla Mujeres, Mexico. Their plan was to cross the Atlantic and return to France. "Hola guapa! We aren't going to France anymore," Valerie replied. "The boat was beaten up on the way to Mexico and we're gutting it and starting over!" She informed me they just happened to be sat at the bar next to an American guy named Richard, who was looking for someone to help him sail to Cuba. Valerie passed Richard the phone, we had a little message exchange and he asked for my email address so he could send me photos of the boat and tell me a bit more about his plan.

The next day I received an email from Richard with photos of him next to the boat. He had a friendly smile and was either really tall or stood next to a very short man. He looked like he was in his 50's, but to be honest, I was still in love with Sebastian and not in the market for a new lover just yet. In his email, he said that he was looking for an extra pair of hands because he had an old race boat that couldn't be sailed solo. His boat was sexy looking with sleek lines, a wide girth and a big central helm. She was white with a red stripe close to the water line making her fast and naughty. I sent the photos to Sebastian, who was impressed and encouraged me to go for it. When I arrived in Mexico, Richard came walking towards me and said, "Wow, you're more beautiful than the photos Valerie showed me." I stifled an eye roll and tensed up with the tiring thought of having to reject his advances. "Thanks," I smiled casually. He showed me to my cabin and left me to unpack my belongings.

Richard remained professional and non-creepy for a couple of days, up until his birthday. Valerie, Robin and I took him out in town for some wild Mexican celebrations. After a sensuous seafood dinner, we drank copious amounts of margaritas and tequila shots.

We stumbled back to the boat well after midnight, positively buzzed from an evening of drinking and laughing. Richard grabbed a couple of beers and invited me to join him on deck. I drunkenly tripped into one of the enormous bean bags and gazed up at the sky. It was a beautiful starry night, which reminded me of the romantic nights Sebastian and I used to have under the twinkling lights. In my drunken mentality, I assumed Richard was interested in my fascinating life story. I droned on about Sebastian and our last year together. Richard abruptly interrupted me, "The best way to get over someone is to stop talking about them and get under someone else," he moved his bean bag closer to me and reached over for what I assume was an attempt to kiss me. I leaned as far away from him as I could possibly get. I was even considering the sea as an escape option if he didn't get the hint. "I'm sorry Richard, I'm just not interested in anyone new right now." He slumped back with a look of disdain, finished his drink quietly and said, "Ok then. I'm off to bed." He stumbled below deck and I sunk deeper into my bean bag, relieved I escaped his claws.

Much to my delight, not a word was said about it again. A few days later, as I was boarding the boat after a yoga class, Richard told me, "Hey, so I'm going to fly in my friend's son to help us sail over to Cuba." "Ok," I replied. "The Gulf Stream can get quite nasty, so it would be nice to have a third person," he continued. "Ok. Sounds like a smart idea, " I replied. The boat didn't have self-tailoring winches, so it usually took two people to work the winches. If the autopilot stopped working, that could make for hard times, and not the kind of hard I like. "He's a lady killer. He's 21 and super hot. He always gets female attention. He used to be a pro hockey player," he carried on. I shrugged my shoulders, "Ok. He's a little young for me!" I rolled my eyes internally. Generally, if a man says a guy is hot, he isn't.

CHAPTER 3

The day of Benito's arrival, I was helping Rodrigo, my 82 year old neighbour re-attach a wind vane that fell off the top of his mast. I knew Benito was turning up any minute, so I declined the kind offer of a thank you beer and hopped over to the steps on the dock. As I did so, my sunglasses fell off the top of my head and into the water. Luckily it was a shallow marina with crystal clear water, so I could see them at the bottom. I stripped down to my bikini and dove in. I grabbed my sunglasses and popped up to the surface. Richard was walking past with, who I presumed to be, Benito. He saw me and said, "Hey! Look who we have here, the marina resident mermaid." I laughed and popped my sunglasses out of the water, "I dropped these!" "This is Benito," he said. "Hey," I said casually and waited for them to keep walking. I didn't want Benito to see what would no doubt be a disgraceful exit out of the water. As I watched them step onto Richard's boat, I thought to myself, "Richard was right, Benito is very good looking, but I just can't be attracted to a man in skinny jeans..."

I hurled myself on to the stern of Rodrigo's boat. "I found them!" I called out to Rodrigo. I stepped off with a firm grip on my sunglasses. "See you later Rodrigo!" I shouted as I walked towards Richard's boat. I hopped on and stuck my head down the companionway. "Hello again!" I shouted. Benito turned around and said, "Oh hey. I didn't realise you were on this boat." "Yep. I'm Brizo. Nice to meet you out of the water." His eyes were an incredible pure deep dark brown. He had taken off his long sleeve shirt revealing the most perfectly sculpted torso that ever passed my eyes. I had only seen a body like that in the movies and magazines. I couldn't wait for him to get out of those skinny jeans, for more reasons than one. I instantly became flustered and went to my cabin to shower and recompose myself.

"We're going to the bar for some lunch. You're welcome to join when you're ready," Richard shouted through the door. "Okay," I replied. I looked at myself in the mirror and thought "You got this woman!"

CHAPTER 4

Richard and Benito wanted to have a boys only dinner, so I kindly accepted Rodrigo's offer to take me out for dinner. The four of us agreed to meet up for post dinner drinks, which meant that my mind was focused on only one thing. How was I going to get Benito between the sheets?

Just as we were taking our last mouthfuls of food, Benito and Richard rocked up to the table. "Hello! How was your dinner?" Richard asked. Unfortunately, Benito was once again wearing skinny jeans, but luckily his eyes were so mesmerising and his arms so perfectly moulded, that I barely even noticed. "Are you going to join us for a drink?" I asked. "Sure," they said sitting down. As we welcomed them into our conversation, I was amused by this overly polite Texan youngster who ends all responses to Rodrigo with "sir."

I seductively sucked on the straw of my cocktail and couldn't help but wonder what magic those arms could do with my body. His muscles bulged out of the bottom of his tight short sleeved shirt. He wasn't like an over muscled body builder, he had pure raw masculine strength. My eyes moved down to his chest. He was part Latino, and his fashion reflected that as he had way too many buttons undone. I wasn't complaining, a warm wet patch was forming in my pants and I could think of nothing else but how he could throw me around. Maybe we could even fuck with him standing up and my legs wrapped around his sculpted torso like I've only seen in movies. I was in awe of his perfection. It was difficult for me to follow the awkward and superficial chat happening at the table as my mind kept wandering to dirty thoughts. He was sitting directly opposite me, so I had the perfect angle to breathe in his ecstasy.

Rodrigo left and Richard suggested we go to a livelier place for a nightcap. We wandered around the loud and colourful streets until we found a place with salsa music blaring and a wall full of different tequilas. He ordered one drink and sat in silence after surrendering conversation to the loud music. Richard quickly finished his drink and said, "I'm going to hit the hay and let you two youngsters carry on enjoying the evening. I can't hear myself think. Just try not to get too drunk. We have a big day of preparation tomorrow." "Don't worry, of course we'll behave!" I shouted over the music. At last! I had Benito all to myself!

We left the bar in search of espresso martinis. Always a bad idea at 11 pm, but I was hoping the night would carry on for quite some time and I wanted sufficient fuel to savour every caress and kiss Benito would hopefully be giving me. We found a cozy bar with a sandy floor and a wall full of whatever kind of alcohol you desired. Coming from inland Texas, Benito was keen to get his feet in the sand, and well, I was keen to get anywhere he was.

We ordered our drinks and perched on the high bar stools. I had already consumed quite a few drinks and my inhibitions were on the floor. I leaned over and said, "Richard said you were really hot. I didn't believe him, but he was right." Without even a blush, Benito put his hand on my knee and said, "When I saw the mermaid in the water, I knew I had to get to know her. It was a bonus when I found out she was the third crew member." I giggled and a flirtatious conversation ensued. After our second drink, Benito leaned in for a kiss, which I happily accepted. That kiss turned me on as much as the first sight of those gorgeous muscles. Red hot waves of passion and lust surged through my entire body, starting a fire of desire in my groins. He took the drink out of my hand and shouted over the music, "Let's go back to the marina." "Not yet, things just got fun!" I retorted. He winked, "The fun hasn't even started. Just follow me."

Benito grabbed my hand and led me out of the bar. We walked down the street with our arms wrapped around each other and my labia swelling with each step. As the streets emptied, he pushed me up against a wall and kissed me with animal raw passion, biting my lip between tongue dances. The alcohol made me forget how insecure I felt around him and I fully relaxed into him. Never in a million years did I imagine this young knockout would be interested in someone that could be his mother. His hand slid up my dress and I pushed him away with a coquettish smile, "Not here!"

I felt like the leading lady in a romance film as we giggled and kissed our way back to the marina. Running through the entrance, I noticed the pool brightly lit in a rainbow of colours. It looked so inviting and romantic and would no doubt be a refreshing break to a steamy evening. "Skinny dipping!!!!" I shouted in a whisper. "Brizo! We can't, it's like 1 am." I hurriedly flung my dress over my head, stripped off my undergarments and jumped feet first into the pool. Condos lined the area, but my excitement made me oblivious. I screamed with delight when I popped back up. "Brizo, shhhhh...come on, someone's going to come out." "I don't care! Come on in. Do you want to have fun or not?!?" "Ahhh, what the fuck..." he mumbled as he removed everything except his boxers and jumped in to join me. I swam in the middle of the pool teasing him with what I imagined was my goddess looking body. He chased me laughing, "I can't believe you're the older one in this situation."

Benito shouted in a whispered voice, "Shit! Someone's coming!!"

I quickly swam to the edge of the pool closest to the walkway. It was a raised pool, so they wouldn't be able to see below my head. As they came closer, I recognised a couple from another boat on our dock. "Hey Brizo. What are you doing? Having a little midnight swim?" I laughed, "Yep, I couldn't sleep!" "Alright, well we're off to bed. Enjoy your evening. Don't stay up too late," they jokingly scolded as they carried on towards their boat. When they were out of sight, I let out a soft giggle and Benito said, "Can we please leave now?!?!" I reluctantly agreed and climbed out of the pool throwing my dress on, carrying my undergarments.

We quietly walked onto the boat, or more realistically, quietly stomped our way to the beanbags at the bow. We clumsily fell back onto the same beanbag, still soaking wet from the midnight swim. Benito wrapped his arm around me and pulled me close to his chest. "This is my favourite bit of being on the water," I proclaimed. "On a night watch in the middle of the ocean, there is nothing more beautiful and more peaceful than a cloudless star lit evening." He replied, "I can imagine. I've never been offshore at night, but the stars are beautiful now." He reached over and gave me a gentle kiss, biting my lip as he pulled away. "I'm cold, I'm going to get some dry clothes on," he said.

The companionway was just above Richard's cabin. We cautiously snuck downstairs and were relieved to find his door shut. We heard him snoring like a baby. I changed into my pyjamas and peeked out into the saloon, finding him lying on his bunk.

"Benito!" I whispered. He looked up, "Yeah?" "What are you doing? Come over here!" His face lit up with a smile as his shirtless body made its way into my cabin. The ceilings were low, so there wasn't much head room above the bed. I crawled in first and Benito followed, climbing on top of me. I took the opportunity to run my fingers over his naked back. It was so solid and firm. I felt his muscles harden and soften as he moved to kiss every inch of my neck. He slid his perfectly chiselled chin and mouth down to my breasts. My pyjama bottoms became saturated with excitement. I yearned for him to take them off and soak up the wetness with his tongue or any other part of his body for that matter. I was totally and utterly his. This was a dream come true. I wanted to savour every moment of this unbelievable experience.

I wrapped my legs around his firm athletic waist squeezing him tight. He worked my body with the same intense concentration of a seasoned sailor perfecting the trim on a sail. There was no doubt he was thinking about nothing else except the body part he was kissing or caressing. The intensity of his passion quickly accelerated my arousal. He kissed and licked my naked chlorinated skin with lust and desire. I was trying not to moan, but it was as hard as his solid cock. I was in absolute sexual ecstasy.

"I don't have a condom, do you?" he asked pulling me out of my deep lustful trance. "No, I don't." I replied disappointingly. The truth is that I did, but I wasn't ready to sleep with my physically perfect man just yet. I wanted to prolong the anticipation of what it would feel like to simultaneously have a hardness deep inside of me as well as on top of me.

His hands sensually tickled my entire body. The Latino genes certainly ran strongly through him if he was that educated about a woman's body at such a young age. Wow! His lips found their way to my nipples and continued south, ever so gently playing with my clit and getting lost in my wetness. "Fuck you are so wet. I want to be inside of you so bad right now," he whispered. I reached over to touch his hardness, but he pushed my hand away and said, "Nope. Tonight is all about you." Wow, really? Is this for real? He must not be human.

I ran my hands all over his irresistibly delicious body. The contrast of soft skin over his hard muscular body was more than I could handle. I quickly reached orgasm and he put his mouth over mine to contain the scream that started escaping from my lips. "Wow," I said. "That was amazing. I can't remember the last time someone made me come so quickly." He laughed. I started running my hands over his body again as I recovered from the mass explosion of pleasure that just occurred. Eventually, I rolled on top of him to kiss his chest and keep going, but he pushed me back down and said, "Another time. Let's get some sleep."

"Ok, but let's cuddle for five minutes before you go back to your bunk," I pleaded. I had already filled Benito in on Richard's advances and we didn't think he would be too impressed about us shacking up together on the first night. He laughed and kissed the top of my head. His arms felt so warm and safe and I felt so small and protected. I fell asleep pinching myself as to how I could be having such an incredible fantasy come to life. I woke up around 7am and heard Richard snoring away. I was about to wake Benito up, but he still had me engulfed in his burly arms and it felt too good. "Just one more minute," I thought to myself as I tried to resist falling back asleep.

CHAPTER 5

We were startled out of our sleeping embrace by the sound of a door being slammed shut. Benito looked at his watch and said, "Oh fuck!" He jumped out of bed and put his shorts back on. He went into the saloon and murmured, "Morning Richard." "I'm just going for breakfast now," Richard muttered grumpily as he walked up the stairs.

I winced and pulled the covers over my head as I knew trouble was ahead. I got dressed and walked out to the saloon, "Shit. I woke up earlier and heard Richard snoring, I really wish I would've told you to go back to your own bed." "Yeah, he is not impressed," Benito said worryingly. "I'm going to have breakfast with him. Maybe you should stay on the boat so I can talk to him." I agreed and followed him on deck. I had absolutely no appetite anyway. I was really looking forward to going to Cuba for the first time and hoped my puma tendencies hadn't closed that opportunity.

About an hour later, I heard Richard and Benito's footsteps on deck. "Good mo-" I said. "Shut it. There are two rules on this boat and both of them were broken. First of all, I said no smoking onboard. There was cigarette ash all over the bow of the boat. " "That was me. Sorry," Benito peeped up. "I said shut it!" Richard demanded. "Secondly, don't sleep with the crew, if anyone's getting laid on this boat, it's me and that's clearly not happening." I stifled a giggle. I locked my eyes on the floor so I didn't look at Benito, as that would instantly throw me into laughter. "Now, I'm going to go sit in the reception lounge and decide whether or not I want you two on this boat." "Ok," I sheepishly replied. "And no fucking while I'm gone!" he shouted over his shoulder.

Benito and I stared at each other in stunned silence. When we heard Richard jump onto the dock, we burst into quiet nervous laughter. "I'm so sorry," he said between giggles. "I should've known better." "Don't say sorry! I enjoyed it, but yeah, that will suck if he throws me overboard." We sat in the cool air conditioning of the boat and chatted anxiously to pass the time.

Benito stated, "He's been gone forever. I'm going to go talk to him and gauge where his thinking is at." "Ok. Good luck," I said. He came up to me with a smile and gave me a sweet peck on the lips, "Don't worry, we'll get to finish what we started. I just have to buy some condoms without him knowing." "Shut up and go see if this trip is even happening!" I replied with a seductive smile.

An hour later, the guys returned. While they were gone, I cleaned the interior of the boat and started making lunch in an attempt to redeem my place onboard. "Right, this is how it's going to go," Richard started. "As I said, no sleeping together. In fact, don't even talk to each other. We're going on this trip because I've been on the dock for seven weeks and I've had enough. It's too late to find new crew now. No smoking and no fucking." "Understood. Ok." Benito and I replied obediently. I let out a huge sigh of relief. "After lunch, the three of us are going provisioning to make sure that we all get what we want to eat." I turned around to hide my growing smile of relief. I still had a chance to finish what dream boy and I started.

Benito and I turned into lovestruck teenagers, forbidden to meet. I sat in the backseat of the car on the way to the supermarket, neither of them talking to me. I dared not enter the conversation for fear that I would never again feel Benito's body. Richard told me to take my own trolley and meet them at the till when I was finished.

When Benito and I passed each other in the same aisle, we exchanged flirtatious looks and turned into giggling school children. Ping! I pulled my phone out of my bag and saw a text from Benito, "This is so funny and weird. I feel like I'm with my Dad. I can think of something else I'd rather be doing right now ;-)" I smiled. It sounded like both Benito and I were hoping to find a way to continue where we left off. The three of us met at the checkout where Benito and I acted as though the other one didn't even exist. Richard appeared happy with the new arrangement and more relaxed.

Back on the boat, Richard prepped the deck for sailing whilst Benito and I stayed inside to put away the provisions and secure the interior. At first, we tried to stay as far away as possible from each other, but it was too difficult. Not only because the inside of the boat was small, but because he was so incredibly irresistible. As he reached over me to put a box in the cupboard, I pressed my body into his and pecked him on the lips. "Oops! Sorry about that!" I said insincerely. He pressed his semi-hardness into me and I giggled quietly. The sexual chemistry between us was bubbling. We somehow managed to behave ourselves in front of Richard and avoided all eye contact and communication when he was in sight.

CHAPTER 6

The plan was to set sail just after sunset. After a quick bite to eat and a briefing of what the watches were, we said goodbye to the neighbours and cast off our lines. I was over the moon to feel the romance of the sea underneath me again. It had been nearly two months since I had been sailing. We were doing solo watches, so I could once again dance to my music under the twinkling stars as the boat danced to its own rhythm of the waves. With the wind conditions, it was expected to be around 30 hours of blissful ocean time.

Benito was incredibly quiet during the sail. When Richard went downstairs for a kip the next morning, I asked him, "Are you alright?" "I'm so seasick. I just don't want Rich to know because he will make fun of me. I keep feeling like I'm going to throw up." "That's shit!" I replied stifling a laugh. I was blessed with the gift of sturdy sea legs.

We had trolling lines on the stern and before I could say more, one of the reels started spinning. "FISH!" we yelled. Richard popped up on deck to help us reel it in. Benito went to the port side to gut and clean the fish. I saw him struggling and asked him quietly, "Do you want me to take over? I really like doing it." He carried on cleaning, "Oh my god. You would save me. I'm going to hurl." I asked him loud enough for Richard to hear, "Benito, can I please do that? I really like gutting and descaling fish." "Are you sure?" My back was towards Richard so I smiled and said, "Please. Come on, just cause I'm a girl doesn't mean I can't touch a fish!" He sat with his back to the winch nearest me and looked at the horizon, no doubt praying for his nausea to disappear.

CHAPTER 7

I woke up half an hour before my watch that evening and listened carefully for Richard's snoring. Never have I been so relieved to be sharing a boat with someone who snored. As long as we were sure he was sleeping, Benito and I could have sneaky conversations.

I quietly crept on deck and said, "Hello!" Nothing. Not even a flinch. Benito was lying down, with his eyes closed, oblivious to the world. I looked around to see if any boats were near us, thank goodness we were all alone! I was horrified that he was sleeping on watch when we were in a busy shipping area. I bent down to kiss the sleeping Prince. He awoke with a startle. I pulled back to avoid any punch he may throw and said, "Good morning. You're not really meant to be sleeping on watch." I once again leaned towards him and gave him a more passionate kiss sneaking my tongue inside of his mouth. He pushed me off, "What are you doing? We're going to get in trouble!" I said, "No we're not. Richard is asleep and he's not on watch for another 3.5 hours. He's snoring up a storm!"

Benito sat up and said, "I'm so sorry I fell asleep. I just felt so sick and I had to lie down and then I fell asleep." "Yeah, it isn't cool," I replied, "If that happens again, please come down and wake me up so I can stand your watch. You'll just have to stay up here and keep me company or do me favours," I winked. He let out a sleepy laugh. I continued, "For nearly two years, I was on a boat where it was just the captain and I. We had all sorts of tricks to stay awake for the 30-40 hour crossing. I was also taught that blow jobs behind the helm are must." He replied,

"Jesus woman. You're naughty. I don't know if I can handle you" I smiled and said alluringly, "I have no doubt you can."

Benito sat up and leaned against the arm rest of the bench in the cockpit. His legs were stretched out in front of him on the seat. I parted his legs and placed myself in between them so I could rest my back against his solid chest. He slithered his perfectly built arms around me and said, "We really shouldn't be doing this. He can wake up at any moment." "I know." I pleaded, "Just five minutes please. This feels so nice and it's romantic under the stars." "That it is," he replied looking up and giving me a tight squeeze. "Do you think Richard will ever let us be alone together again?" I asked. "Hmmmm...probably not to be honest," replied Benito. My heart sank, but I wasn't giving up hope just yet. He kissed my neck and squeezed me tighter.

CHAPTER 8

We arrived in Cuba just before sunrise and waited for the morning light to guide us through the treacherous reefs that surrounded the entrance to the port. We had sailed to the most westerly tip of Cuba, which was barren and windy. There were a few short trees that had been shaped to a slant by the constant strong winds, a square brick building, which I presumed was the immigration office and another little building with a thatched roof and some tables outside. The sky was showing off her morning glory with shades of pink, purple and orange. Our arrival was a bit anti-climactic to the vibrant, loud and colourful Cuba that I had conjured up in my mind.

There was no supermarket, beach or town anywhere nearby, so we went to the restaurant, which was disappointingly closed and waited for our passports to be stamped. Benito and I awkwardly ignored each other. I wouldn't put it past Richard to leave me stranded here. I was more than capable of getting myself to civilisation, I just didn't want to risk being stripped away from the gorgeous young stud. My mind wandered off to thoughts of how I would devour Benito when it was just the two of us.

At last, the clearing in process was complete and we were allowed to sail off to our first destination. Richard was an avid speargun fisherman and the idea was to sail around the south side of Cuba snorkelling, spear fishing and enjoying the incredible peace of the isolated bays. It would've been the perfect romantic sailing trip if it was just Benito and me.

After a few hours of champagne sailing, we arrived in a beautiful bay and dropped anchor to swim and eat a late lunch. Richard was so much happier and relaxed. In between mouthfuls of pasta he said, "You guys can talk to each other, you know." Benito grumpily said, "Yeah ok, thanks." I didn't say anything as I found the whole situation comical. But at last, the tension was broken and we could carry on as a "normal" crew who talked and looked at each other!

Richard, Benito and I snorkelled around the nearby reefs. The guys wanted to spear a fish or three for dinner. I didn't really want to see any of it, so I went off on my own. Not long after I swam away from them, I felt a little tug on my fin. Startled, my heart started racing in fear it was one of the many barracudas that were stalking me. I turned around and saw the beautifully sculpted chest of Benito, which sped up my pulse even more. I waved at him and he motioned for me to follow him. He led me to a lively colourful coral full of fish. We popped our heads above water. "There's a huge lobster down there, but I don't know how to get him. Give me some tips." I went down and searched for the lobster who was hidden in a crevice. He was huge! We resurfaced, "How do I do it so he doesn't go further in the crevice?" "Cross your fingers and give it your best aim!" I giggled. "If I catch him, should I pull the tail off and drop the rest? I'm worried a shark might get us." I laughed and rolled my eyes. "There is more to the lobster than the tail and it's cruel to do that. There aren't any sharks which will attack you in these waters," I said. "It's the stalking and vicious looking barracudas you have to watch out for." "I'm already getting chased by one," he said flirtatiously. I rolled my eyes and reinserted my mouthpiece.

~ 26 ~

We dove down together and I watched him take aim - pssshhhh - the arrow shot forward and Benito missed. I gave him a thumbs up as he swam up for air. "Fuck! Now what?" "He hasn't moved, so just go down and shoot again." He looked around for Richard, who wasn't anywhere to be seen, and pulled me in for a kiss. I wrapped my legs around him and wouldn't let go, "Good luck!" I said as I soaked in more kisses before pushing him away.

This time, he had a lucky shot. He popped up to the surface very excited, with his prize in tow. We swam back to the boat, showing Richard the catch as we swam past him.

Richard joined us at the boat a few minutes later with a lobster and a red snapper. Everyone was in good spirits for the first time since "the incident." It was impossible not to be happy in these spectacular surroundings.

After eating a fresh seafood dinner I didn't have to cook, Richard said he was tired and was going to bed. Score! Alone time with Benito! We took the beanbags up to the bow and stared up at the stars. Benito said, "I really need internet or WIFI. Just before we lost signal, I got a message from one of my friends about an epic birthday party next weekend." "Why would you want to go there, when you have this?" I asked. Benito said, "It's my best friend's birthday, I don't want to miss out." I said, "You'll miss out on this, and me." "Yeah, like anything is going to happen between us with Rich around." "We just have to get creative," I smirked. He laid back and closed his eyes. I worried that the secret romance was ending before it even started.

CHAPTER 9

The next day, our sails took us further East to another breath-taking bay. This time there was life onshore with a huge resort and busy beach bar. Finally!! Maybe we could get some private time without fear of Richard looking over our shoulders or interrupting us at any moment. "Do you think the bar is open?" Benito asked. Richard replied, "Why do you care? We have enough alcohol onboard to open our own bar." "I just want to get on land," said Benito. While they had their little discussion, I went for a swim. I really didn't care if I was going to land or not. The motion of a boat rocking on the waves had become my norm over the last year and I was happy to be in harmony with the water again.

"You guys get out of my hair and go to shore. Have a drink and food if they have any," Richard said to us cheerily. I looked at him mischievously, "But I thought we weren't allowed to be alone." "Ahhhh, I don't care anymore. Just go off and have fun like youngsters are supposed to." I could barely contain my excitement as I ran to my cabin to get ready. I followed Benito into the dinghy, Richard shouted, "Hey, Benito, let Brizo drive. There's less of a chance something will get broken." I laughed as Benito sulked and moved over to give me control.

The beach was absolutely beautiful with fine white sand and a line of palm trees rustling in the breeze. The sun had already set and Mother Nature was wearing a seductive robe of deep purple, dark red and a hint of pink. I grabbed Benito's hand as we walked along the beach towards the bar. The air was filled with the scent of fried food, promising something for dinner and more time alone together.

Benito ordered a few drinks and we sat on the beach talking freely whilst enjoying the sky tucking itself in for the night. Benito quickly downed all of his drinks. "I'm going to get more, do you want another one?" I looked at him, "What's wrong? Why are you drinking so fast and looking sad when we're in paradise?!" He put his head down and said, "I came here because I'm running from things. I love cocaine and I just needed to take a step back because I'm spending $3000 a month on coke and I don't want to anymore." I was shocked and sad to think he had such dark demons that he was running from. He carried on drinking the whole night and telling me his short, yet difficult life story. Always attracting the men that need saving, my hopes of picking sand from in between my bum cheeks were quickly shattering.

We moved to the bar area and a little kitten started playing with Benito's legs. He leant down and picked it up, "Where is your mother little one? Or are you just like me, orphaned with no one to care about you?" I didn't think it was possible for him to dry my loins, but I was wrong. After some time, I said, "Look, let's try to cheer you up. There's nothing you can do about anything right now. Let's go back to the beach." I was hoping a change of scenery would snap him out of it and that lying down on the sunbeds at night with the moon rising over the water would direct his mind back to my body.

I was out of luck that night. When we got to the sun loungers on the deserted beach, Benito started crying. I hugged him tight and let him release liquids from a different orifice. It was getting late, so I drove us back to the boat to a happy Richard.

He must have enjoyed time alone in the way that I was hoping to enjoy Benito.

The next day, Benito was awkward around me. When Richard went to shore, Benito said, "Look. Forget everything I told you last night. Don't ever mention it again to me or anyone." "Don't worry," I said, "your secret is safe with me." Then he carried on talking about needing to get to this party and wondering when we were going to get be near a bigger port so he could leave.

CHAPTER 10

We arrived in Cayo Largo del Sur and docked in a marina, ending the romantic days of morning swims in beautiful bays. Benito sniffed out the nearest airport and booked the first ticket back home, which was in three days. Richard tried to talk him out of leaving so soon. "Man, it's only been 10 days. You can stay as long as you want. That party is one night and you probably won't miss out on anything. There was no convincing Benito. He had his mind set on the party and was already checked out of boat life. "Oh well," I thought to myself, "At least I had a little bit of fun."

Richard seemed keen to sleep and spend time on his own, which gave Benito and I plenty of time to explore the tiny little island we were stuck on until he left. Much to my demise, he continued to be distant and rarely laughed unless he had the right amount to drink. One afternoon, we met an American guy who had also randomly hopped on a boat to help the owner sail. His name was Nick and he had a similar story to mine, albeit he was 10 years younger than me. As he was on his own, we invited him to tag along with us. It was a welcomed break from Benito's silence.

The night before Benito left, the three of us crew went out for a farewell dinner. After we finished eating, a couple of our neighbours, including Nick, asked us if we wanted to join them for drinks. Richard said, "I don't think so. I'm tired, but you guys go ahead. Just stay out of trouble." "We will!" we shouted in unison. One by one, the people we were drinking with went back to their boats until eventually it was only Benito and I, along with a few unknown people sat around the bar.

Despite my growing desire to feel Benito inside of me, we managed to develop a trusting friendship. "Why do you have to leave?" I asked him quietly, "I actually really like you. Although I don't think I'll ever meet anyone that will put up with me forever," I scoffed.

"Brizo, you're like gold. One of a kind. Everyone wants to have a bit of gold. But then people get gold and they don't know how to maintain and care for it and they leave it. But don't worry, there's someone out there who knows how to polish gold. You'll find him." Feeling extra emotional because of the alcohol, my eyes welled up with tears and I reached over and gave him a huge hug. His powerful arms squeezed me back and made me feel so safe and cared for. Exactly the feeling I was seeking. His genuine soul and kind words made my mind go straight to the gutter. My heart wasn't the only thing I could feel pulsating.

I had given up hope that we would finish what we started between the sheets. I was really going to miss Benito. Not only was he absolutely gorgeous, but I treasured the time we spent together. He had a unique and innocent, but wise view of life that I could listen to for hours.

One of our neighbours, Sofia, was at the bar and called us over. She was hilarious. It was clear that she had been drinking for quite a while as she told us the woes of what it was like living with her captain. They were "banging," but as time went on, she didn't want to fuck him anymore and was desperate to get off the boat. I joked that my time on the boat was probably coming to an end, so she should meet my Captain. "What's he like?" she asked me in her heavy Russian accent, "I've seen him around and he looks ok." "He's nice and easy to live with. He's really good at sailing. I think he would be happy if you cooked more than I did!"

Benito put his rock hard arm around my waist and whispered in my ear, "Look, I'm tired and I have to wake up early. Let's go back to the boat." "Ok, no problem. I probably don't really need more to drink anyway!" I replied. Oh that arm around me...it made my brain turn to mush and I became putty in his hands. I desperately wanted to get lost in his arms one more time and feel his lips delicately caressing every part of my body. It seemed so cruel being given the opportunity and then having it stripped away from me as soon as it happened. We were so close, yet nothing more was to happen.

As we headed back to the boat, Sofia shouted after us, "Don't leave! The night is still early!" "Fuck," I muttered under my breath. We were hoping to sneak away without her noticing as she had become bolshy and annoying. "We'll be back!" we lied.

She ran after us and said, "I come with you. I want to go to my boat and pee." Benito and I gave each other a look and then carried on walking. As we got to our boat, she slurred, "Oh yes, maybe I meet the captain now." I shook my head, "No way. He's been asleep for hours and it's the middle of the night. Wait until tomorrow."

Benito jumped on the boat and reached his hand out to me. I grabbed it and jumped into his arms. "Good night! See you tomorrow." Instead of leaving, Sofia followed me on the boat. I stopped and said, "Sofia, look it's not a good idea, I don't want to get in trouble. If you really want to get on a different boat, you need to leave now and meet him in the morning."

She pushed past me and went down the companionway. She started shouting, "Where is the Captain's cabin?" I ran down after her and quietly said, "Sofia, get off now. It's not the time." She proceeded to open up the door to Richard's cabin, "What the fuck is going on?" screamed Richard. Benito came to the rescue and forced her up the stairs, "Get out now. You weren't invited on the boat."

Richard came out of his cabin and looked at me, "What the fuck did you do now? Why did you invite her to the boat?" I stared back at him in disbelief. "She just barged on to the boat," I said defensively. "I told her to come in the morning because she wanted to talk to you." "Yeah fucking right," he murmured as he slammed his door.

Upset, I went on deck and saw Benito had managed to get Sofia on the dock, but she was pushing her way back onboard. "Come on Brizo, let's take her back to the bar and have a drink so she gets away."

I stepped off the boat and took her arm to direct her back to the bar. "No, I do not want drink. I want Captain," slurred Sofia. "Get away from the boat! You're drunk. Just leave us alone!" I shouted angrily. She escaped from my grasp and stormed onto the boat. Benito ran after her and much to my horror, she started towards the companionway. I came running after her, but before I got a chance to grab her, she had pulled up her skirt and her underwear down and was pissing on the hatch,

"No, no, no, what the fuck are you doing? Are you crazy? Why would you do that?" I shouted at her in a whisper.

"I'm going to get her captain, this is fucking crazy," said Benito. I was completely helpless. The only thing I could do was watch her relieve herself on the entrance to the boat, praying that Richard would stay inside. I was hoping to watch some relief tonight, but not that kind. She finished peeing, stood up, looked me in the eye and said, "I piss on all of you," and started laughing maniacally.

The captain of her boat stomped down the dock, "Sofia! Come here right now!" he shouted. He apologised to us and said he would make sure she would stay on the boat until the morning. Benito grabbed the hose and rinsed the piss away. I knew that Richard was going to chuck me off the boat because he blamed the whole incident on me. In my drunken state, I burst into tears and ran off the boat. "Brizo! Just wait," Benito called after me.

I ran off to a part of the marina which was still under construction. There were no boats and it was free from pedestrian traffic. I sat on the dock with my head down, hugging my knees and sobbing my heart out. I was going to lose Benito and the boat and I didn't know where to go. I felt the floating dock moving and heard heavy footsteps. I looked up expecting to see the security guard, but instead, Benito's silhouette grew larger as he came towards me.

He sat behind me, put his legs on either side of mine and wrapped his solid arms around me. He kissed my neck and embraced me tightly. "Come on, it's going to be ok. I'll talk to

Rich and tell him it was my fault. Don't worry." I proceeded to cry harder, "I don't even have anywhere to go if he kicks me off. I can't go back to my parents and I just don't have money to go anywhere." "Ssshhhhh. It will be ok. Don't worry," he reassured me. He continued to hold me tight while I emptied myself of all the sadness.

Eventually I cried myself out. Benito kissed my neck and squeezed me tight. "Come on, let's go back to the boat and get to bed. I'll make sure it's all sorted out before I leave tomorrow." He was truly a knight in shining armour and I was devastated that he was riding off tomorrow. I accepted his hand to pull me up and threw my arms around his neck.

Not only did he feel so strong and safe, he smelled so good. It instantly awakened my sexual appetite. When we arrived at the boat, I went into my cabin and he to his bunk. I laid there feeling sorry for myself. Not only was I going to have to devise a new plan, the hottest guy on the face of the earth was on the other side of the wall and I never even had sex with him.

A few minutes later, Benito opened the door wearing nothing but his sexy boxer shorts and said, "So... it's our last night, are we going to fuck or what?" I moved over to make room for him and giggled, "Only because you were so romantic about it!" My wishes were finally coming true!

He seductively slithered into bed next to me and kissed me slowly and passionately. His fingers ran through my hair and he pulled my head to the side as he kissed the side of my neck. "Oh my god. Wow," I whispered while wrapping my legs around him. His tongue protruded from his lips until they found my breasts, his strong hand firmly grabbed the back of my neck. His lips floated over my chest, torso and down to my hips, kissing them gently to increase the moistness between my legs. He sailed further south, stopping to nibble on the inside of my thigh. I grabbed his hair as I made a silent moan. No way was I going to risk waking Richard up right now. Nothing was going to interrupt my dream coming true.

His tongue slowly circled my clit. Both of my hands grabbed his hair and showed him a rhythm that would prolong the pleasure. His touch felt so good and I didn't want to orgasm too soon. I pulled his head up to my lips and said, "Fuck me now." Without using our hands, his hardness found it's way into my soft, wet pussy. Our bodies danced together as if we had been making love for years.

We started off slowly and gently, speeding up as the passion intensified. My hands revisited his gorgeous firm terrain. I wanted to touch every centimetre of his skin and feel his solid body move as he pleasured me. I was drowning in pleasure and before I realised it, I started to orgasm. My back arched and my breasts lifted towards him. The release was unexpected and incredibly intense. I was dizzy with pleasure and my body had melted so much that I could no longer be an active participant.

"Can I come yet?" asked Benito. "Hmmm...yes, you can," I gasped. His thrusting became more intense as he had his own release. He laid down breathless and sweaty next to me. I draped my arms and legs over his glistening physique. He held me for a few minutes, squeezing me and giving me gentle kisses on my head. "I better get back to my bed. I think we're already in enough trouble." I agreed and gave him one last squeeze and kiss. "Good night!"

CHAPTER 11

Richard awoke before us. I heard him leave the boat and breathed out a sigh of relief. I wouldn't have to deal with his grumpiness first thing. After all, I hadn't done anything wrong. I walked into the saloon to find Benito sleeping profoundly. He looked so gorgeous with his leg resting on the back of the sofa and his perfectly sculpted arm over his head. I sat at the edge of his bed and gently bent down to give him a kiss, "Good morning!" He grabbed me and pulled me down on to him. "Where's Rich?" He asked. "I don't know, I heard him leave the boat." "Good. I wonder how much time we have until he yells at us." It wasn't long before we heard his heavy footsteps walking above on deck. I jumped up and went to the galley to make tea.

"Good morning, what the hell happened last night?" he asked with a smile on his face. Benito began explaining, "That girl is mental. She came on to the boat even though Brizo and I told her to go away. I woke up her captain and told him to get her. He said she had some mental issues when she drinks." Richard laughed, "Yeah, I know. He saw me leave the boat today and came running to apologise. He's flying her home in a couple of days because he can't take her craziness anymore. Don't worry about it." My shoulders fell with relief, I wasn't going to be kicked off after all!

Richard left to find a taxi. I gave Benito a big hug and pinched his bum. "Call me anytime you need to get away from things," I said. "Thanks for all the fun memories." I gave him one last kiss, full of passion and followed him off the boat. I waved goodbye and went to find Nick so I could tell him all the juicy details and relive the most wonderful sexual night of my life to date.

JUAN

CHAPTER 12

Richard and I carried on sailing east along the southern coast of Cuba. He wanted to sail to Cienfuegos, stopping along the way before heading South to Jamaica where I would leave the boat. I was ready for a new adventure now that Benito had left.

After spending a couple of nights in quiet anchorages and enjoying early morning snorkels, we sailed into the port of Cienfuegos. The channel was dotted with traditional Cuban fishing boats filled with eager fishermen hoping to bring in a good catch. They welcomed us with waves full of spirit as we sailed towards the rising sun.

Green lush trees dotted either side of the channel until we turned right and the town popped into view. The horizon ahead of us was filled with smoke stacks and high-rise apartment buildings. Both sides of the channel were lined with run down shacks protecting its occupants from the falling elements with palm leaf roofs.

As we approached Cienfuegos, we saw a bunch of sticks poking up to indicate the location of the marina. I was hoping to meet some nice people as Richard already informed me his mission was to find himself a prostitute to help him with his ever increasing sexual tension.

As we approached the dock, I threw our lines to the young marinero who didn't speak a word of English. I happily translated, while my mind worked to find an escape plan. When everything was settled, I asked Juan in Spanish, "Can you please take me out with your friends one night and show me how Cubans live? I need a break from the captain." Juan laughed, "Yes. I finish work at 8 tonight and I will meet up with my friends around 11. I will pick you up at 10." I bounced back on the boat and told Richard that Juan invited me out with his friends that evening. "That's great," he replied uninterested.

When I woke up from my nap, Richard said, "I met one of our neighbours who knows where to take me to find a nice girl, so don't wait up for me." "Ok, cool. Have fun!" I said trying not to vomit. I wasn't disgusted that he was getting a sex worker, I just didn't find Richard sexy in any way and the thought of him heaving awkwardly on top of a gorgeous Cuban woman was beyond disturbing. I immediately started imagining him clambering around in the bedroom and it wasn't a pretty image. He's probably a surprisingly great fuck, but I had no intention of finding that out for myself.

Juan arrived early, wearing jeans and a nicely ironed button-down shirt. He greeted me with a huge smile that took up most of his face and showed off his pearly white teeth. He was much taller than me and very skinny. He wasn't my usual type, but I appreciate a good looking man no matter what the colour. "Just give me one minute to get ready," I said hurriedly. When I came back out, Richard was using the opportunity to practice his less than basic Spanish. No doubt he was getting ready to converse with his future Cuban lover. I wished him a fun evening and rescued Juan from the laboured conversation.

Juan was a gentleman, opening the marina gate for me and inviting me to walk through first. "Please correct me when I say things wrong and teach me Cuban slang!" I told him. He stuck to his word and we giggled at some of the rude phrases he taught me. It was a long walk into town, made longer with the slow crawl we set in order to manage the hot, muggy evening air which made my skin glisten.

After what seemed like hours, we arrived at the malecon. "I came to get you early so we could drink a beer on the wall and talk," he said. He was an intelligent 27 year old wise beyond his years, which made for interesting conversation. We discussed philosophy and life in general, which made for a refreshing change from the drunken sailing stories Richard shared. We had a fascinating conversation and before I knew it, an hour had flown by and a group of his friends were walking towards us. His body may not have stirred my loins, but his mind sure was.

"Oye!" Juan and his friends greeted each other. He introduced me to everyone and I instantly forgot all their names expect the only other female, Matilde. She was holding hands with a skinny, yet muscular guy with a chiselled face and gorgeous smile. Lucky her. They started speaking to each rapidly in a Cuban accent, so I stayed quiet, listening for the odd word I may understand. We arrived at the discoteca just after midnight. Sweat dripped down my cleavage in the hot sticky night and the club was quickly filling up with dancers. The Latin music vibrated from the speakers and the walls lit up with a rainbow of colours from disco balls dangling from the beams. I looked up and discovered it was roofless, revealing a beautiful starry night.

Matilde, her husband, Juan and I danced the night away. Juan was a somewhat awkward dancer. He preferred to dance by himself against the wall, stepping in place and dancing with his hands. This didn't give me hope for his bedroom skills, if I was that way inclined. It was obvious Matilde's partner was a professional dancer as they contorted their barely clothed bodies in sexual acts, to the beat of reggaeton. They seamlessly spun to the rhythm of salsa and bachata. As Juan wasn't an engaging partner, I looked around and watched the local women in sexy scantily clad clothing, bodies dripping with sweat, dancing with tall gorgeous, chiselled men. The dancing was so intimate and sensual I felt like I was in a sex club watching an orgy. Eventually the disco lights faded, bright white lights lit up the dance floor and the music abruptly stopped.

Juan asked if I wanted to go for a swim with Matilde and her husband. "Sure," I replied. We walked to the shore and Matilde and her husband stripped down to the bare minimum. Juan and I shyly did the same. The water felt so cool and refreshing on my overheated skin.

We swam out until we couldn't touch the bottom anymore. Matilde and her other half swam further away from us. Juan came close to me and we treaded water together. As we chatted, I looked over and noticed that Matilde was making interesting thrusting movements. "Are they???" I whispered quietly to Juan. "Probably," he laughed. "Wow, I guess if they're married, they have to practice making babies." I shrugged. "They aren't married. They just met tonight," I laughed quietly, "Really? But he said..." "I know," Juan said. "He likes to pretend stupid things." Juan came closer to me and reached in for a kiss. I was going to resist, but the rum told me that I was only in Cuba once. Juan tried his luck by attempting to pull down my underwear, but I wasn't interested. I swam away from him and said, "Sorry. I'm not like Matilde."

Juan apologised profusely and we swam in awkward silence for a while. "I should really go home now," I said. I had no idea what time it was, but I guessed it was around 4 am. I heard Matilde's non-husband coming to a climax. I looked at Juan and laughed. As we hopped onto shore they shouted, "Wait for us, we're ready to go too," Matilde shouted. "I bet they are," I whispered under my breath laughing. Juan walked me to the boat and I gave him a hug goodbye.

CHAPTER 13

Richard's plans were to leave for Jamaica the next day, but some bad weather was about to come in and the Coast Guard prohibited any boats from leaving port. Looking at the weather forecast, it would likely be some time before the wind would blow our sails south. Richard found a girl who satisfied his needs, so he decided there was no rush in leaving.

"I'm tired of sleeping in that cramped bed. I'm going to get a hotel room for a couple of nights," Richard told me one afternoon. "I know you and Juan are good friends now, but no Cubans are allowed on the boat," he said. "If the police find a Cuban on the boat, even in the marina, I'll go to jail. You guys can hang out, but it has to be on the dock." Despite having 37 years to mature, I mischievously thought to myself," Did he just challenge me to have a Cuban on the boat? I think he did." "Understood. Not to worry Rich," I assured him falsely.

Juan was on the overnight shift that evening, so I invited him round for pasta. "Are you going to be around for dinner?" I asked Richard. "I'm going to make some pasta and Juan is coming over, should I make enough for you too?" "Nah, that's ok. You can have a romantic little dinner on the dock. I'm going out to eat with Natalia." "Ok, have fun." I replied.

I made pasta with tomato, onion, olives and tuna. Juan was amazed with the meal. "I normally just eat pasta with tomato sauce," he exclaimed. In fact, he had never eaten olives before. "Mmmm.. que rico," he moaned between bites. "You better stay out here while I wash the dishes," I said to Juan. "That's ok, I will go check in with my colleagues." "Maybe I will tell them to keep a look out and I can come and see the inside of the boat?" he asked with a sparkle in his eye. "Great idea!" I winked.

I finished washing the dishes and waited in the cockpit for Juan to return. My star gazing journey was interrupted by footsteps on the dock and I sat up. He was back. "Hola!" I said. "Sigue." He stepped on the boat and we dashed inside in hopes that none of the neighbours would see. I didn't think they would call the police, I just didn't want them ratting me out to Richard. We sat down on one of the saloon sofas, "Thanks for dinner. I've never had those things. They are delicious. It was nice to try something new," he repeated. "My pleasure," I replied.

Juan reached over and kissed me. His hand quickly travelled up my shirt and he groped my breasts over my bra. He squeezed with soft quick pulses. I didn't have much faith this was going to go well, but I live to break rules, so I went with it. "We should hurry because I don't have much time," he said. To be honest, I wasn't really that interested in having sex with him. I was thinking of Benito anyway, so the quicker the better I suppose.

He unbuttoned his work trousers and I pulled the underwear down from underneath my dress. He sat down and pulled me to go on top of him. "Do you have a condom?" I asked. "No sex unless there's a condom." I replied. "Si, si, si. Espera." He dug in his trouser pocket for a condom and put it on a semi-flaccid cock. I internally rolled my eyes. "Te ayudo?" Can I help you? I asked. "No, todo bien," he replied.

I placed my knees on either side of him and straddled him as he leaned on the back of the sofa. He attempted to shove his soft cock into me. It was no surprise that it wasn't working. Juan pressed my hips down on to him, but he kept slipping out. I was finding this absolutely hilarious. I wanted him to give up and get out, but he acted as if everything was fine as he whispered Spanish sweet nothings into my ear. "Que rico, mami," he repeated (The Spanish use the term 'Que rico' for everything from food to fun to sex).

I couldn't even tell if he was inside me at this point, but he's verbally acting excited, so I make the noises that one is supposed to make and pray to the semen gods for a quick ending. What felt like hours, but probably only minutes later, he grunted and jerked his body then dropped his head back onto the sofa. "Viniste?" Did you come? he asked me. "Si, si." I lied. I normally don't lie as that won't help me achieve an orgasm with a regular partner, but I knew a next time didn't exist. I just wanted him to leave so I could erupt with laughter. During this sexual experience (if you can call it that), I had the feeling that Richard was going to come back and I didn't want to get caught. Especially as it wouldn't have been worth it!!

"Que rico Mami," he smiled as he put his trousers back on. I slid my underwear up and accepted his goodbye kiss. I went out first to see if anyone was around. I signalled that the coast was clear and he jumped back on to the dock. He blew me a kiss and wandered off to carry on with his shift. I laid down in the cockpit and laughed quietly to myself. What the hell was that?? How did he even come when he wasn't hard? I would've thought he was lying, but it definitely looked like there was liquid in the condom when he took it off. He took it with him, so I couldn't even investigate. Ew, did I really just think about looking in the rubbish for a condom?

I gazed up at the stars, stifling giggles at what had just happened and wondered what Benito was doing. Oh, how I missed him and his company. He would've thought this story was hilarious. I fell asleep in the cockpit and woke up abruptly to a heavy footstep on the boat. I shot up in a panic. When I opened my eyes, I realised that it was Richard. "Jesus, you scared the living shit out of me," I said. "You're not the first person to refer to me as a religious figure tonight," he smiled. "Oh yeah, then why are you here?" I asked. "I had enough and just wanted to sleep alone," he said. "Ok, well good night," I said sleepily. I checked the time on my phone. It had only been 45 minutes since Juan left. My intuition was right about Richard coming back!

The next morning, the dockmaster came to the boat and told us that the weather was clearing and the port was open again. "You better say goodbye to your little lover. We're out of here," Richard said. "He's not my lover," I said as I rolled my eyes. We did one last supermarket shop that day, cleared out and Juan came to throw us our lines. As nice as he was, that was certainly one line I didn't mind being untied.

CHAPTER 14

We set sail for Jamaica. I was ready to get out of Cuba and Richard was ready to get me off his boat. When we arrived, the marina manager, who I knew from my first visit to Jamaica, caught our lines. After we were securely tied up, I spoke to him privately. "Hey Tony, do you know of any boats going to Panama?" I asked him. "Yes, there is one actually. They pulled in yesterday." He pointed to the motor yacht. "Thanks Tony!" I walked over to the boat and asked to speak to the captain. "I'll have to think about it as we already have a full crew," he said. "Come back in the morning and I'll give you an answer."

I hopped back to Richard's boat with a positive feeling that I had discovered my escape vessel. Sure enough, the next morning the captain said they would happily bring me to Panama. "You can move aboard immediately if you like because we're looking at a 5am departure," he added. Sebastian and I had been separated for two months and I realised I wanted to be with him. I was looking forward to being showered once again with affection and orgasms.

BACK TO SEBASTIAN

CHAPTER 15

I spent one more year with Sebastian before the owner decided to sell the boat. To our pleasure, he wanted to sell the yacht in Florida and asked if we would deliver the boat there. The trip would take 10 days and would be the last sailing adventure Sebastian and I had together.

The wind was on our beam the whole way and we had a perfect sea state making for smooth sailing. The days were warm enough that we could go uncovered and feel the wind on every part of our bodies. We laid together in the cockpit kissing and caressing each other's bodies as the mood took us.

One day when I was taking a salt water shower on the stern, I heard a cry and turned around to see if Sebastian was ok. He came running out asking if I was ok. "I thought that was you," I said with surprise. The swell was bigger that day and we scanned the sea to investigate if it was our imaginations or someone needing assistance. As a wave rode up, we saw a man on a homemade canoe waving his oar in the air. "Do you think he needs help?" I asked. Sebastian replied, "There are fishing boats over there, I think he came from one of them." I said, "Let's get close and give him some coffee for a fish!" "This is borderline pirate territory," he replied. "Best not to stop." I asked him to bring me my towel as we sailed nearer to him. We waved and carried on with trepidation wondering if the fishing boats were actually pirates who may make an unwanted visit.

That evening, I was anxious about pirates, so Sebastian slept outside while I did my watch. As we swapped watches, I said. "Look how amazing the stars are this evening!" We lied down so we could watch the twinkling sky. Sebastian's sailor muscles wrapped around me and I snuggled into his chest.

The romance of it all stirred up a yearning in between my legs. Despite the chill in the salty air, I took off my trousers, undid Sebastian's shorts and slid on top of him. I rolled my head back to glance at the stars. My hands slid up his shirt to feel his soft skin and gentle muscles. His hands gently grasped my hips and we let the momentum of the ocean guide our rhythm. As we knew each other's bodies so well, we could easily climax at the same time. Which is exactly what we did that night. As he reached his peak, Sebastian looked into my eyes and called out "Que rico!" while I showed him just how much he pleasured me with a loud moan.

SUPER YACHT LIFE

CARL

CHAPTER 16

After Sebastian and I sailed into Florida, I went back to London and completed all the necessary courses to get a job on a super yacht. Within a week of completing, I was on a plane to St Martin to start my first job. An incredibly sexy French sailor was sat next to me and asked me my story. I had a glorious seven hours of being entertained by his tips, escapades and charming smile.

I was sat in the window seat and as we approached St Martin, an island he knew very well, he leaned over and started explaining the layout of the island. I felt the warmth of his breath as his body leant into mine. I turned to look at him and noticed the sneaky glance he gave to my lips, as if he wanted to taste them. Oh, how I wanted him to put his hand on the back of my neck and give me a proper French kiss. Sadly, it didn't happen, but he gave me his number so we could stay in contact. "If this is super yacht life, I am 100% in!" I thought to myself with a cheeky grin.

I had no idea what I was getting myself into. After having a blissful two years running the boat with Sebastian, I was expecting relaxation, occasional hard work and lots of bikini and water time. I was in for a shocking surprise. On my first day of work, I was instructed to clean things that already looked extremely clean to me, but I went with the flow and was an obedient crew member.

I quickly sussed out the crew and took a liking to Carl, the engineer/deckhand, who was young and hilarious. He was in his early 20's and exuberated a false sense of confidence enhanced by his brunette military style haircut. On deck, he spread out his muscular broad shoulders and puffed up his well-built chest whenever a pretty woman walked by. He grew up in a completely different world to me and I enjoyed his quirky sayings and young fresh perspective on life. The Captain, Grant, was in his 50's and whilst we got along, I was more inclined to connect with a younger energy.

The crew very much liked their drinking. At that stage, I barely drank alcohol. I went out with the crew a couple of times to be social, but they drank hard and fast. I made my excuses to leave early so I could wake up for my daily dose of yoga and meditation. They all thought I was weird, but I didn't have the desire to drink anymore. I felt lonely and out of place. It was so different to living and working in a quiet and peaceful harmony with Sebastian.

The itinerary was intense, working six days a week with no guests and loads of drama when they were onboard. Over time, Carl and I realised we could trust each other and vented about whatever drama was unfolding in front of us. After releasing our rant, we fell into hysterics about something totally unrelated and all was ok again. Occasionally, Carl asked me to help him with something in the engine room. He normally didn't need any help, he just used it as an excuse to give me some relief from the guests constantly calling my name. A close relationship quickly ensued between us, making the rest of the crew suspicious about what we were getting up to when we went off alone.

It didn't take me long to be swayed by the masses. One evening I broke and got drunk with everyone. Back at the boat, Carl and I smoked a joint together on the top deck. The weed sucked the words from my mouth, leaving us sitting in silence as we admired the stars. "So should we have sex then if it's been such a long time for both of us?" Carl asked. "Yeah right. Grant told us the crew weren't allowed to fuck each other," I reminded him. "We just do it and not tell anyone," he replied with a cheeky grin. "Carl, I could be your mother if I had you as a teenager. That's just gross." "What!?! No it isn't, you're a MILF and I'm not your kid." The sexual spark was ignited, but nothing happened that night.

Manuela, the chef was sex crazy. Her most frequently spoken phrase was, "I miss dick so much, I need dick in me now." Often this sparked story time about each of our crazy sex adventures. One day when Carl, Manuela and I were watching TV, Manuela suddenly asked Carl "Can you whip out your dick please?" Without blinking an eye, Carl replied, "Only if both of you girls show me your tits." We looked at each other and shrugged our shoulders, "Ok," we responded. He took out his dick and Manuela lost all control, "Oh my god!" she screamed in her Mexican accent. "Oh my god! It is so big! I want to suck on that big dick!" He laughed and put it away. "Ok, now you girls go." After teasing him that we weren't that crazy, we both flashed him for about two seconds. Manuela couldn't stop talking about his dick and how "beautiful" it was. "Enough about his dick Manuela. If they're too big, it just hurts after a while," I replied dismissively.

One Saturday evening, everyone was out except Carl and I. Carl walked into the crew area where I was. "Go out you loser. You're young. The woman of your dreams could be out tonight," I urged him. He was half dead with a hangover and said, "I can't even stand up, much less hold a conversation with the woman of my dreams. She'll have to wait." Carl came back from the toilet and sat next to me. "I get so horny when I'm hung over, do you?" asked Carl. I rolled my eyes, "Yes, but I'm not hungover." "Come on," he egged on. "We're all alone on the boat." "Yeah, and what happens when they come onboard and we don't hear them?" I asked. He pointed to the video screen above the TV. "There's only one way on and off this boat. We just watch the camera while we get busy." He unbuttoned his shorts, whipped out his cock and stroked it while looking at me. "Carl!! Put it away! Besides, if you really want to woo me, sticking your dick out and expecting me to sit on is not the way to get in my pants." He rolled his eyes, "I'm too tired today." I stood up to go to my cabin. "Where do you think you're going?" "To my cabin so I don't have to deal with your shit." He stood up and put his arms around me, trapping me so that I couldn't escape. "What do you think you're doing?" I smiled back at him.

Carl gave me a peck on my lips and nibbled on my bottom lip. I gave him an unimpressed look. "Is this what you wanted?" he asked. "Not at all. I'm not even wet yet young man. I've seen the size of you, he's not going anywhere near her until she's properly lubricated." His horniness overrode his tiredness and he lifted my shirt up to do undo my bra. "Ok, but who's going to watch the camera? I don't want to get fired," I repented. "We'll take turns. I can't watch it while I'm doing this," and he started to suck on my nipples. I was slowly warming up to the idea, so I let him carry on, half hoping we would be interrupted before it got too far.

Let's just say Carl's strength was not foreplay. He was an amateur in the sexual world or perhaps just incredibly selfish. He pulled my shorts down and laid me down on the crew bench. "Ok, now you have to watch, I can't see the camera," I said. He fumbled around with a condom and eventually manoeuvred his way inside of me. Just as I was accepting his short and fast thrusts, he came. My devil's doorbell stopped ringing and a wave of disappointment passed over me. This is what I get for accepting his advances?! He redeemed himself when he slid his hand in between my thighs to give me some attention.

All of the sudden he jumped back and reached for his clothes, "Shit!! They're coming!" "Yeah right," I said. "Perfect way to get out of having to make me come." I sat up and looked at the camera. "Oh fuck!!" At this point they were already in the cockpit stubbing out their cigarette butts. I quickly put my clothes on and did up my bra.

We sat on opposite sides of the table to make it seem as though we were casually watching a movie. They came down and the captain said, "Oh, I'm surprised you guys weren't fucking in one of your cabins." I rolled my eyes and said, "I wouldn't even think about touching Carl." Carl laughed out loud and said, "You wish you could have this tasty piece of young meat." The captain and deckhand said good night and went to their cabins. Carl and I looked at each other with open mouths in disbelief and started laughing. "I'm going to bed. Good night," I said.

The other crew continually teased Carl and I about an imaginary sexual tension. "It must be so hard not to be able to fuck when you want her so badly Carl." It clearly wasn't there, as the tension had been broken! He rolled his eyes and said, "She's a bit out of my age range." "That's the kind of woman you need, she can teach you a few things and Brizo, you can have a man with fast recovery time!" Grant teased.

CHAPTER 17

As I wasn't impressed with Carl's sexual capabilities, I was in no rush for a repeat performance. Plus, there were some hot guys in the marina I wanted to meet. "I didn't get a chance to show you my skills," Carl said whenever he was horny. "It's fine, we've been there, done that and can move on," was my standard reply. After being with a man who had more years of sexual experience than Carl had on this earth, I wasn't keen for another round of selfish sloppy awkward sex. Despite nightly attempts at going out to get laid, Carl was never successful, therefore his persistence was relentless.

Most nights, Carl and I sat on the top deck to appreciate the magical night sky. Carl usually smoked a joint and I occasionally had a puff. One evening in which I indulged in the green goddess, he scooted closer to me and pulled me towards him. "Should I tell Bill that I'll cover his watch for him so we can be alone?" Carl asked quietly. "Whatever you want to do Carl." I laughed. "Yes, I'm going to get lucky!" he said as he jumped up. He went below deck to have a word with Bill. I laid on my back to observe the stars and have a private conversation with myself. "What would be the worst that happens if we try again?" I asked myself. After all, I was super horny and the prospect of getting caught added to the excitement.

Carl ran back up to the top deck, "Bill is going out to meet Grant," he exclaimed excitedly. "Nice," I smiled. I went into the cockpit to smoke a cigarette so I could see when Bill left. "See you later Bill. Have fun!"

When he was out of sight and earshot, I went back up to Carl, "The coast is clear!" I sat next to him waiting for him to finish his joint. "It's such a beautiful night. I love living on a boat. We get to see and access so much more than people living on land," I said. "Yeah, it's pretty fucking cool. The best part is that we even get paid for it," he replied. He put his hand on my leg and started rubbing it up and down. "Ooo... am I going to get some foreplay this time," I joked. "You're lucky you get any piece of me!" he retorted. I rolled my eyes and shook my head in response.

When Carl finished, we went to the crew mess to keep an eye on the cameras. Without a word, he pulled me onto him and gave me a slow and passionate kiss. Mmmmm...he may have come quicker than a hurricane rips the sails off a boat, but he certainly knew how to kiss. I felt a moistness developing between my thighs. Luckily, I didn't have to wait long to be touched as he unbuttoned my shorts, let them fall to the floor and popped me up on to the crew mess table. I wrapped my legs around him and unbuttoned his shorts. "People eat on this table," he said. "I know. It will be our inside secret," I winked.

He scooped me off the table and turned me around. "Bend over," he demanded. "Oooooo... yes sir," I replied coyly. I bent over the crew table and waited for him to push himself deep inside of me. It wasn't hard with his size. I was wet and ready to be fucked. He gently entered me and let out a moan of pleasure. "Oh god," he sighed. His rhythm increased quickly and once again before I knew it, he was coming. "Seriously?!? What the fuck Carl? Again! You still haven't made me come!"

As I turned around to look at him, I glanced at the camera. The captain was stepping onto the passarelle. "For fuck sake. I miss out again. Fuck you Carl!" We hurriedly put on our clothes and he went into his cabin. "How was your night?" I asked Grant as he came into the crew mess. "Boring. I'm getting too old for this shit. What are you up to?" "I was just about to go to bed," I said. I was hoping that the sheer disappointment of another one-minute sex session wasn't written all over my face. The worst part about it was that I shared a cabin with Manuela and I didn't dare do the job properly on myself, in case she returned to the cabin mid orgasm.

The next day Carl was late getting up for breakfast. As he stumbled out of the head to sit down at the table, he looked at me and we both stifled a giggle. Bill's plate was at the exact spot my bare ass had been the night before. The captain rolled his eyes, "What's going on now? Can you guys just fuck and get it over with already?" That made us laugh even harder.

CHAPTER 18

"Carl. It's not on that you've had two orgasms now and I've had NONE!" I protested. "In fact, I've hardly gotten any pleasure at all with the amount of time you last." He laughed and said, "It's your fault for taking so long."

The next time we were alone, I was determined to claim what was owed. Carl was lying down watching TV and I walked up to him and unzipped his shorts. "Oh hello!" he smiled. I undid his shorts and slowly started licking his girthy shaft up and down. "You're going to make me come this time, no matter what," I informed him as I took the tip of his hard stick into my mouth. "Whatever you say as long as you don't stop," he groaned. I played with his cock in my mouth for a good few minutes and when it seemed like he was about to come, I stopped. "I'll finish you off after I get what's coming to me."

Carl quickly got up from the bench, "Take your shorts off and lie down." I did as I was told and his fingers found their way inside of my already juicy pussy. His other hand wandered up my shirt to play with my nipples. It had been a week since the last time we had sex and my sexual appetite was building. "You're so wet and ready," he said with excitement. He took his hand out from my pleasure zone, "What are you doing?" I asked. "I'm going to fuck you." "No you're not. I know what happens when you fuck me. First you're going to finger me until I come."

His finger returned to circle around my clit, "Tell me how to make you come," he whispered. "I'll tell you if you're doing it wrong. Just keep going." I replied. He was certainly hitting the right spot. I felt myself getting wetter and wetter, my breathing intensified and my back arched with pleasure. "Don't stop," I moaned. "I'm almost there." The speed and pressure of his finger increased, driving me wild inside. I felt the blood rushing to my pussy and focused on nothing but the pure state of bliss I would soon be experiencing. I felt my lips swelling, my legs relaxing and my body getting ready for orgasm. Finally! I was nearly there, "Oh my god. Yes, keep going... I'm coming." The climax was intense. It had been months since I had been touched by another man and the eruption was overdue. I felt a wave of pleasure move throughout my whole body.

"Now can I fuck you?" he said. "Have you been watching the camera?" I asked. We both looked over and much to my amusement and Carl's despair, Manuela was walking into the cockpit. Once again, we hurriedly threw our clothes back on and I walked towards my cabin as if nothing happened. Finally, the tables had turned and no matter how hard he begged to keep playing, I was walking away from the game.

ADAM

CHAPTER 19

Whilst nothing more happened between Carl and I, he was still kind enough to give me a lovely birthday present. "I want to introduce you to a guy even *I* have a crush on. He's a pilot for private planes," Carl said. "I'm interested and listening," I replied. "Tell me more."
"I'll tell him to come to the bar tonight and you can find out for yourself," he said.

After a special birthday dinner, we went to the marina bar which was just steps away from our yacht. Adam was already there. He spots Carl, smiles and waves. "Wow, you're right Carl. Look at that smile!" Adam was tall and slender with a bald head, striking blue eyes and a warm smile that lit up the bar. "Brizo, Adam. Adam, Brizo," Carl introduced. "You guys want a drink?" My intention was to have a sober evening, but this guy was hot and I was nervous. "Sure, I'll have a birthday beer," I said. "It's her birthday Adam. She's single, so if you can think of a gift...." he said as he walked off. Leave it to Carl to leave with an air of uncomfortable silence.

We chit chatted until Carl returned with the drinks and broke the tension. "Let's play pool with these guys," Carl said to Adam. When he wasn't shooting the pool stick, Adam stood next to me. "Am I allowed to ask how old you're turning?" he asked. "Sure, I have nothing to hide, 37." "Honestly?!?" he exclaimed looking me up and down. "You look great! I wouldn't have guessed you were even 30." "Thanks," I smiled. Even if a guy is lying, it's still flattering to hear. "So, what are you doing here? Working on a boat or a holiday?" I asked, pretending that Carl hadn't told me anything. "Neither. I'm a pilot and I flew my boss over here where he keeps his boat for the winter." "Very cool. How long are you here for?" I asked. "I fly back tomorrow," he said. Just my luck. He was my age, super good looking and probably great in the bedroom. Of course, he wouldn't be around for long.

As the night wore on and they were beaten at pool, Adam leaned in and asked me, "What do you want for your birthday?" "To wake up on a sailboat like I've done the last two years," I said without hesitation. "Oh really? I happen to be sleeping on my friend's sailboat. I have the boat to myself, so I could make your birthday wish come true." For real? Maybe luck was on my side after all. My eyes sparkled and I laughed, "Really??" "I don't tell a lie." He put his arm around the small of my back. "Jesus girl, you're rock solid, are you a body builder or what?" he asked. "Nope, I'm just a sailor," I winked back. Carl interrupted us, "Brizo, we have to go back for your birthday cake. Grant just messaged to say they're waiting for us."

We went back to the boat where the crew, a bunch of crew from the surrounding boats, and Adam sang me happy birthday with a cake full of fire. As Manuela cut a piece of cake for each of us, I glanced at the clock and noted it was 11 pm. My birthday was nearly over. I was anxious to go to Adam's boat and be alone with him. "We're each going to give you 37 birthday spanks," Grant said. "Then you can say you got gang spanked on your birthday." The crew mess erupted into laughter. I kept sneaking glances at Adam and willed this part of the evening to be over so I could feel the sensation of his hands all over me. As I took my last bite of cake, Grant shouted out, "Now go have a happy birthday and get fucked." The crew on boats know everything and Carl obviously told him that he had a friend for me. "Fuck you Grant," I said laughing. I grabbed Adam's hand and practically ran off the boat.

We hopped in Adam's dinghy. I sat next to him, my heart beating rapidly with anticipation and my vagina throbbing from his hand high on my thigh. We clambered aboard the sailing boat and Adam gave me a quick tour. The final part brought us to the master cabin where Adam was sleeping. "Wow! This is even better than I could have hoped for!" I exclaimed. The cabin was the width of the whole stern and there was a slightly bigger than double bed in the middle of the cabin. Windows spanned the width of the wall at the head of the bed. Even though the view was the dock, it was a beautiful cabin. "Oh yeah, is it alright for the birthday princess then?" he said as he came over to wrap his arms around me. "For sure," I replied as his lips met mine with a surge of passion. He opened his mouth and our tongues introduced themselves. I let out an involuntary gasp. His hand travelled up the back of my neck like a man who knew how to pleasure a woman. After Carl's cute and overexcited attempts at trying to please Mrs Robinson, this was more like it.

With each kiss, Adam shuffled us closer to the bed. He placed his hand behind my back and gently lowered me to the bed. The soft lapping of the waves on the hull and the rocking of the boat mixed with his zealous touch instantly sent me into a state of deep relaxation. He sat up and removed his shirt. Wow, what a sight. There must be a gym in that cockpit. He had a beautifully sculpted chest and strong muscular biceps. I breathed in the sight of his chiselled torso and barely even realised sounds were escaping his lips. "Sorry?" I said as soon as I realised his lips were moving. "Can I take your shirt off too?" he smiled. I laughed and sat up. He pulled my shirt over my head and gently pressed me back onto the bed. He slipped one hand underneath my back and effortlessly unclipped my bra. "He's certainly a pilot!" I thought to myself.

Waving away the thought of him with countless other women, I turned my focus back to his thrilling touch. His hands slowly and confidently explored my body. I felt as though I was a newly discovered treasure being examined carefully so as not to be broken. My hands explored his tight muscular back and caressed those perfectly sculpted biceps. Strong arms make me melt into putty. I found my way to his belt buckle and he squirmed away, "Mmmm, mmmm birthday girl. You first." As much as I wanted to explore every part of him, I was also happy to lie back and enjoy whatever gifts he wanted to give me.

His hand led the way from my neck to my swelling breasts as his lips and tongue followed. The mixture of sensations created by his hands and mouth sent electric tingles up and down my body. Adam placed his mouth over my nipple and alternated between sucking hard and softly. I wrapped my legs around his waist to prevent him escaping from this tantalising task. He turned his attention to my other nipple. They were standing to full attention, that's for sure. My hips wriggled from side to side, ready to receive any part of him. I felt a humid heat surging between my thighs. I desperately wanted him to touchdown on my private airport.

After acquainting himself with my now fully perky bosom, his finger traced a line down toward my stomach, followed by his mouth. I craved for his finger and mouth to carry sailing south, but instead he tacked to the sides of my abdomen. Oh he was such a tease! He finally continued on a southern route, but skipped over my pulsating flower and down to the inside of my thighs. Waves of tingles and pleasure surged through me. At last, his talented tongue found its way to my magic button. My hands reached for imaginary hair on his bald head as my body slithered wildly with delight. The confidence he exuded placed me completely at ease and I came in about 20 seconds. "Happy birthday," he muttered. "Happy birthday to me. Wow, that was a great present," I exclaimed short of breath.

Adam slid up next to me and wrapped me in his arms. "You alright?" he asked, kissing the top of my head. "Mmmm...yes, definitely. That was really intense and I'm overwhelmingly satisfied," I muttered. I don't know if Adam had any other intentions for that evening, but it remains a mystery as both of us fell asleep.

The sunlight creeping through the windows on the east side of the boat gently woke us up. "I have to go," I said sleepily. "My birthday is over and it's back to work." Adam very coldly said, "You want me to bring you in the dinghy or do you want to walk?" I was a bit taken aback by his abruptness. "What time is it? I don't think I have time to walk along the road." "Alright then. Just give me a second."

He left the bed and went to the head. I heard water running as I put my clothes back on. He came out about five minutes later. "Let's go then." He pulled alongside the boat and hung onto the yacht as I climbed up. Grant and Carl were in the cockpit with a knowing smile. I looked down and said, "Safe flight. Thanks for a good birthday," I said flirtatiously. I was so confused as to his total change of demeanour. "Yep," he said not even looking at me. When I went into the cockpit, Carl asked, "So how was it?" "Why are men such dickheads?" I replied as I walked towards my cabin.

BASEM AND MATTHIEU

CHAPTER 20

The full moon was high in the sky, sexily shimmering off the water in front of me. The vibrations of the bass from the techno music playing in the background were pumping through my body. A warm breeze passed through my Caribbean curls warming up my cool tanned skin. I heard French and English voices competing with the music, sounds of laughter and people having a good time. I had been in St Martin for a month now and I had just begun to relax to the Caribbean vibe. Carl asked if I wanted to join him and his friends at a full moon party on the beach. "Sure, why not?" I replied.

We arrived to faint sound of music filling the salty air. The bass of the music started vibrating through my body as we approached the party. Disco balls hung from the palm trees throwing a mix of colours onto the soft white sand. As the others in my group said hello to friends, I stood back and inspected my surroundings. I was quickly approached by a French guy. "You are beautiful. Your smile is like a ray of sunshine." I giggled, "Thank you!" It sounded so sexy with his French accent. He pulled his friend over, "Look at this beautiful woman. Look how perfect she is and that smile." His friend agreed and bent down on one knee, "Yes. Will you marry me?" I laughed nervously and said, "I don't know yet. Maybe!" At this point, two other guys noticed me and turned to look at me. One of them came up behind me and put his arm around me, "Wow. Perfection. Those eyes!" I became slightly uncomfortable by this sudden flurry of attention. Carl walked up to me. "Are you alright?" he mouthed to me. I shook my head no. The French guys said, "Oh, you with him? Wow. Lucky man. I want to marry her." Relief swept over me when Carl said, "Come on. Let's get a drink." "Wow. I guess I know where to come if I ever feel unattractive!" I said leaving my admirers behind to pick up their fallen jaws.

I followed Carl and his friends to the shoreline. We sat down to bathe in the moonlight and hear each other speak. Four guys in their late 20's walked over, drawn in by the smell of weed, "Do you mind if we sit with you?" they asked in a foreign accent. I said, "Of course not, have a seat." They were also smoking a joint and passed it my way. I politely declined, but was happy to have new people to talk to.

Two of the guys lived on their own boats and chatted away about their sailing adventures. We had a lovely evening dancing under the stars. One of the guys asked me for my contact details before we left, but I wasn't really expecting to hear anything from him.

The next day I was surprised to receive a message from Basem. He was a young French Algerian living and working in St Martin. He was tall with friendly eyes and a warm smile. I remembered being encaptivated by his conversation and thinking what a shame it was that I didn't have any sexual attraction towards him. "It was nice to meet you last night. Would you like to go out with my friends and me some night?" I eagerly expressed my interest as they were the first interesting people I had met who were here for longer than a day.

Basem picked me up the next evening and took me to a hotel bar where his friend worked. They were all French so I couldn't understand a word they were saying. The hotel was right on the beach and I focused my attention on the mesmerising waves as they crashed on the beach in the moonlight. One of Basem's friends came up to him at the bar and ordered a drink. "Brizo, this is Matthieu. He speaks English," Basem introduced.

I was instantly captivated by Matthieu's stunning green/grey eyes. He was wearing athletic clothing which hid his skinny, yet muscular body. It turns out he was a tennis coach and had just finished a lesson. I spent the best part of the next hour working out if he was shy or a stereotypical arrogant French guy. "Where did you learn English?" I asked. "I lived in London for a while and had English girlfriends," he replied. "Always the best way to learn," I replied with a wink. He said something to the bartender in French and I was again left to the side of the conversation. I discreetly observed him. His eyes were absolutely stunning, but he was a bit thinner than I preferred. He was a tennis coach after all, they are not known for their stocky build. He had a gorgeous smile that was mysterious and seductive. I tried a couple of times to engage him in conversation, but he responded with quick answers before continuing his French conversation.

The hotel bar closed at 9 pm. Matthieu asked Basem if he wanted to go somewhere for another drink. "Brizo, would you like to come with for another drink or should I take you back to your boat now?" Basem asked me. "I'm happy to go for another drink. The night is young!" Basem said something to Matthieu in French and then turned to me. "Matthieu has to go home and change, let's go with him." "Ok," I said and followed them out the door.

Matthieu's place was next door in an old hotel that had been transformed into studio apartments. There was a double bed, a sofa, a little kitchen area and a bathroom. While we waited for Matthieu to shower and get ready, Basem introduced me to Ricard. It's a French liqueur drunk with the perfect amount of still water and it's delicious! Matthieu was impressed that I liked it and gave me that award winning smile. "You are almost French now, no?" "Mmm...how I would like a bit of French in me now," I thought to myself.

Matthieu took out a little bag filled with white powder, "Do you want some?" he asked me. "No thanks, I don't do that anymore," I replied. In his sexy French accent he said, "Do you mind if Basem and I do some?" "No, not at all." He poured some onto a little coaster and cut it up with a credit card. They asked me, "What do you want to do tonight?" "I would love to go dancing!" I replied. "Ok, I think I know the place," said Basem.

Matthieu topped up our drinks and we sat on the balcony smoking cigarettes and chatting about travelling. When we finished our drinks, Matthieu and Basem stood up and started speaking in French. "Hey," I said. "Not fair. I don't know any French!" They apologised and told me, "We were saying that we need more cocaine, but I don't know if you want to come with us because it's a proper ghetto. Is that ok?" "Sure," I said. "Why not? I'll get to know the real part of St Martin."

We left Matthieu's studio and piled into Basem's 4x4. Driving in St Martin, or in the Caribbean for that matter, is a thrill-seeking experience one never knows if they're going to survive. High speeds on narrow curvy roads with lots of speed bumps turn me into a believer of God as I pray for good brakes and a strong neck.

As we approached the drug dealer's neighbourhood, Basem turned to look me in the eye, "Ok. Now where we're going, just don't be scared. It may seem scary, but it's safe. Sometimes there are guns, but only for protection." "Ok, sounds exciting!" I replied, admittedly a bit nervous. The fear increased as we drove down a dark narrow street with beat up tin shacks for houses. Music blared loudly from different houses and groups of mostly black men congregated on the street smoking all sorts of things.

Traffic built as cars shared the roads with more and more pedestrians. Basem waved at someone and stopped. He rolled his window down and said, "Hey man, where is Stinty?" "He's at home mon, go ahead," he replied nodding his head forward. As we drove further into the ghetto, the pot holed road became an uneven bumpy dirt road with more and more intimidating looking people following our car with their eyes. "Don't be scared. I promise you're safe with us," Basem assured me. I laughed. I wasn't really that scared. I've been around the block plenty of times to understand that the drug dealers aren't going to harm their regular customers. It was clear from all the waves and nods of acknowledgment that Matthieu and Basem were known around here.

The dirt path ended and Basem pulled up into a parking area. "Do you guys want to stay in the car or go with me?" Matthieu said, "I'll stay in the car with you if want me to Brizo." I was feeling quite adventurous that evening, "No, let's all go." We walked down a tiny narrow pathway filled with people. Reggae music blared from various shacks lining the path. Most of the doors were open allowing the harsh lighting of bare bright light bulbs to creep out into the pedestrian path, lighting our way. The air was pungent with the smell of marijuana, mixed with scents of fried food.

The lane was lined with conjoined shacks made out of tin and plywood. There was no way a private conversation could be had in this neighbourhood. Each shack had a door, but most of them didn't have any windows, providing some physical privacy. Their occupants roamed outside drinking beer or cuddling up to their partner. I smiled at them, said hello and casually glanced into the open doors.

It was the kind of thing you see in movies. Dirt floors, what looked like old broken chairs and tables, makeshift kitchens and a curtain separating what I presumed was a bedroom or bathroom. I have to admit, I was a little wary of being the only three white and foreign people, but I kept calm and confident and smiled at everyone as I walked past. Most of the time a polite smile was offered back.

At the end of the path, Basem stopped and talked to a guy standing outside of a door. They spoke in French, so I didn't understand what was being said. The guy reached his arm out towards the door, indicating that Basem could go in. Matthieu and I waited outside and the guy looked at me and said, "Go ahead, go in." I followed Basem and went into the shack.

It was a small square room with a table and three chairs. A black guy sat at a disfigured metal table. Two guys stood behind him like bodyguards. With a joint in his mouth, he nodded his head at Basem and looked me up and down. I smiled and said, "Hello." The guy sitting down said something in Creole to one of the guys behind him. This guy went behind a curtain and came back with a small bag of cocaine. The dealer offered Basem a taster from the bag. He looked at me and I smiled. "Sorry, only one taster." I was relieved because if I said no, he may think I'm undercover and I really didn't want to say yes. Basem took a line and nodded his head. The dealer gave Basem the rest of the bag and another smaller one. We left the shack and looked for Matthieu. He was further up the lane talking to someone in French. I was relieved that we were leaving and so far, still alive. Back in the car, Basem turned around and said, "See! I told you that you would be safe with us. Were you scared?" "A little bit!" I proclaimed honestly. Him and Matthieu laughed, "Unfortunately we are regulars so they know and trust us." "The dance club isn't opened yet, so let's go to a bar first. You can get another Ricard down your throat." "Sounds good to me!" I said.

CHAPTER 21

Matthieu and Basem introduced me to the bartender, who was gorgeous. His long brown hair was tied up in a ponytail. I started daydreaming about being naked with him and grabbing that ponytail as he worked magic between my thighs. His smile and eyes were so inviting and sexy that the only thing I could say to him was, "Hi."

It was that in between time where the responsible crew had gone home for the evening, but the late-night partiers weren't out yet, so the bar was nearly empty. We took a seat at the bar and ordered our drinks. "I'm going to the toilet," I said. "Do you want to bring some Charlie with you?" Basem asked. "No thanks, I'm good."

On the way back, an attractive tall blonde-haired guy came over to me. "Wow. You are gorgeous. Where are you from?" "England," I replied. "Do you want to dance with me?" I quickly realised that he was off his face on something, as many people in St Martin are. "Not right now thanks, I'm chatting with my friends." He said, "Oh let me meet them!" He followed me over to the bar and I introduced him to Basem and Matthieu. I was trying to talk to them, but the tall guy repeatedly asked me if I wanted to dance and go home with him.

Basem could sense my annoyance, so he waved me closer to him. "Are you ok?" he asked. I said, "No. He just came up to me and now he won't leave me alone." "Is it ok if I put my arm around you and then maybe he will leave?" Basem said. "Yes of course. Please do!" I felt his arm gently wrap around my waist and give me a little squeeze. The drunk guy came up and said,

"Oh, are you with him?" "Yes, I am." He tried to speak to me some more, but Basem just turned around and gave him a threatening look. The drunk guy gave me the name of his boat in case I changed my mind later. As hot as he was, being that fucked up really isn't attractive. I mean, would his dick even function?

The Ricards were going right through me and I needed the loo all too soon again. The drunk guy saw me and ran up to me. "Hey, where are you going?" "To the toilet!" I said in an annoyed voice. "Ok, I'll come with you." "No you won't!" I snapped. I opened the door and he held it open about to come in, "Please leave me alone now. I don't want you in here." He started to argue with me when the bartender approached us. He grabbed the drunk guy and shouted, "Get out of here. If you have a penis, you don't belong in here!" I quickly peed and walked out of the bathroom. Basem was standing outside. "Are you alright? The bartender told us what happened." "Yeah, I'm fine. Thank you so much."

I thanked the bartender, who poured me another drink. "Sorry you had to experience that. It's not the first time he's done that tonight." My ego only slightly bruised I wasn't the only one, I thanked him again and carried on chatting with Basem and Matthieu. Basem looked at his watch. "The salsa bar is open now. Let's finish these drinks and go." "Yay!!!" I exclaimed.

On the way to the salsa bar, I realised just how tipsy I was. I had no idea where in St Martin we were. We seemed to be driving in circles, yet ending up in different places. It had been a long time since I'd had more than couple of drinks in an evening and I was enjoying the loose, carefree and confident sensations the liquid courage was giving me.

We arrived at the club and were the only three white people. It was ladies night, meaning I got two for one drinks, just what I needed at that point! I ordered a drink and gave my second one to Matthieu. Basem asked me if I wanted to dance. He was an excellent salsa dancer and spun me around the dance floor. After a few salsa songs, the beat of the music changed to reggaeton. A few local women came near us and started twerking. I tried imitating them unsuccessfully and everyone around us started clapping and laughing at my attempt. "Teach me how to twerk!" I shouted into one of the women's ears. I tried a few times, but my stiff hips made it an entertaining sight for everyone watching. Luckily, I have no shame!

"Come on." Basem said. I followed him and Matthieu outside, where I thought we were going to smoke. They got into the car and I said, "Well that was fun!" Basem replied, "We're just going to do a line, I don't want to leave you alone in there." "Oh, ok!" They offered me a line and I declined. "It's been five years since I've done that stuff. If I managed to live in Colombia for two years without doing it, I think I can keep going."

After they took a couple of lines each, we went back into the club. Basem and I once again stole the dance floor to show them how white people can't dance. A local tapped on Basem's shoulder and asked if he could dance with me. "Is that alright with you Brizo? You don't have to," "Sure," I said. He stood nearby as we danced, watching me the whole time and giving me the occasional thumbs up. After some time, Basem said, "Matthieu wants to go because he doesn't like to dance. Let's go to another place." "Ok!" I said. I was drenched in sweat and getting tired anyway.

CHAPTER 22

Before we pulled out of the car park, Matthieu cut up some more coke. "Are you sure you don't want a line? It's really good stuff." I had drunk enough for that to sound like a good idea and said, "Ok, just a little one then." I did half the line he cut for me, "Holy shit, you weren't kidding, that is some really good shit!" I snorted the other line in the opposite nostril and sat back. The familiar sensation of invincibility and confidence surged through my sweaty body.

After the dance club, we stopped at the beach where some of their friends were having a small party. Following that, we went to the local strip club, only because it's one of the few places open past 1am. We made another quick trip back to the ghetto because Matthieu had lost the bag of coke somewhere in the strip club. This time I stayed in the car with Matthieu.

Before I knew it, it was 5 am and we're walking into another club. Basem tapped me on the shoulder and pointed across the bar. Much to my despair, the tall drunk guy that followed me into the bathroom was standing at the bar. When I went to the toilets, Basem followed me and waited outside. "Just in case," he said.

As I left the bathroom, Basem was standing there with a concerned, yet relieved look on his face. "Everything alright?" he asked. I smiled and gave him a big French kiss. After all, he was French. The coke, alcohol and rollercoaster of emotions I felt that night came crashing together for a recipe of mischief.

As we were kissing, Matthieu came up behind me. Basem pulled me to his side. "I'm jealous," Matthieu said. I turned around and gave him a kiss too. "There. Now you don't have to be jealous." Matthieu slipped his arm around my waist and Basem slid his arm around the other side of me. Basem pointed to an empty sofa at the end of the bar. "You two go over there and I'll get us another drink." "I don't think I need one!" I shouted after him.

Matthieu sat down and I straddled him, kissing him passionately as if we were in our own private little love nest. Basem came back with two beers and I leaned away from Matthieu so he could take his beer. Basem sat down, reached over and pulled my upper body towards him and kissed me. My lips travelled between Basem and Matthieu for I don't know how long. One or both of their hands ran up and down my body, making me extremely turned on. "Let's go to the beach and watch the sunrise!" I exclaimed. I jumped off Matthieu and we left the bar.

"Looks like we missed it," said Basem. "I don't care! Then let's go for a swim!" We had no idea what time it was as Matthieu and I had left our phones at home and Basem's had died. I had to work at 8 am, but the elation I was feeling of meeting people I connected with, mixed with the invincible feeling cocaine gives me, made work the least of my worries.

We were the only ones on the beach. "Do you want to have a threesome?" Basem asked us. Matthieu and I looked at each other and shrugged our shoulders. "Ok," I said. Matthieu started taking his clothes off as Basem kissed me and pulled my shirt up. I saw a guy walk from a beach house and sit about 10 meters from us. "I think this ends here," I said and pointed over to the guy. "Hey, do you know what time it is?" Basem asked the guy. "It's 7.30," he replied. "Shit! I have to go," said Basem in a panic. "My Dad needs my car for work. I will be right back!"

I asked the local, "Is it ok to go topless on this beach?" The guy replied, "Do whatever you want to do honey." I stripped down so that I was only wearing my underwear trimmed with lace. I ran into the water screaming out with joy and Matthieu followed. I dove into the lukewarm, salty water. When I popped above the surface, I exclaimed, "This is what life is all about! I'm soooo fucking happy right now! I have to start work in half an hour, and I don't give a fuck!!" I laughed and floated on my back. Matthieu came up to me and pulled me towards him. He gave me a passionate kiss as I wrapped my legs around him. I could feel how hard he was and swam away. I was too involved in this moment of ecstasy and freedom to want sex. I again floated on my back and Matthieu swam between my legs. He moved my underwear to the side and circled his tongue around my clit. I closed my eyes and relaxed. This is the life. What a different life I was living to three years ago. I vowed I would never return to work behind a desk.

Matthieu was nearly drowning as he carried on tickling my oyster. I had gone past the point of horniness that coke usually gives me. I let him carry on half drowning as he licked away. The warmth of his tongue felt amazing next to the cooler temperature of the saltwater surrounding my body. Eventually I stopped him and said, "I should really get to work. I'm pretty sure I'm late." "Ok, I will walk you to the marina. Then I will figure out how to get home since I don't have a phone or a car and I don't think Basem is coming back." Luckily the marina was only a five-minute walk from where we were. I didn't have a towel, so I threw my clothes over my wet body.

CHAPTER 23

I gave Matthieu a goodbye hug and kiss at the gate. "Thanks for a really fun evening," I said. "I hope we can do it again soon." I gave him another smooch. "Yes, it was very fun. I want to see you again," he replied. I walked through the gate, waving one more time before walking to the boat. I had a huge smile on my face as I floated to the boat without a single thought of possible repercussions from Grant as a result of my fun and wild evening. When I approached the boat, I saw Grant and Bill in the cockpit smoking. I waved at them and casually walked onto the boat.

"Do you have any idea what fucking time it is? Why the fuck didn't you call me. I've been trying to get a hold of you. All I knew was that you were going out with some Algerian. God knows my imagination was running wild as to what he was doing with you. Are you alright?" shouted Grant. "Yes, I'm fine. Sorry I didn't call, I left my phone on the boat." "Why the fuck are your clothes all wet?" "I went for a morning swim," I said quietly. "What have you been doing? Take off your sunglasses." "I'd rather not. It's bright out here." I replied. "Take them off right now," he demanded. I slowly removed the sunglasses and looked down. "Look at me!" he shouted. I looked up at him, "Jesus fucking Christ, I expect this from Carl because he's still a child, but not from you. You're in no condition to be working today. Go to fucking bed." "I can't. I want to work." I protested. "You're not working. Now get inside."

I reluctantly went to my cabin to shower and change. I put on my uniform and went into the saloon. Grant was there making a coffee, "I don't know why you put your uniform on. Do you want a coffee?" Before I had a chance to respond, he said, "Stupid fucking question. Of course you don't, that's the last thing you need right now," and snickered to himself. "What the hell happened last night?" I knew he was asking out of concern because most of the time the other crew went out, him and I stayed behind in the crew mess chatting about life. "I don't know. I haven't done coke in five years and they made it sound good, so I tried just one line and it was really good, so I kept going." He gave me a hug and said, "Hey, it's ok. We all make mistakes. You fell off the wagon and you can get back on it."

"I really should fire you. Especially because Carl pulled the same overnight late for work shit you did, and I told him I would fire him if he did it again," he scorned. "I'll give you another chance because I like you and I don't think you'll do it again. Just know if you do, I will have to fire you on the spot." "Ok, Grant. Thanks so much for understanding and giving me a chance." I made myself a tea and went to sit in the crew mess. I managed to fall asleep mid-morning and woke up after lunch. I had missed calls from both Matthieu and Basem asking me if everything was ok with my captain. I messaged them, "All is fine."

That evening after everyone was done working and I could come out of hiding, Grant received a phone call from the owner saying we needed to take the boat to St Thomas immediately, because her friends were flying there and she wanted to take them on a cruise. My heart dropped as the previous evening's adventures with Matthieu and Basem ran through my mind. Luckily, she only wanted to go on a one week trip. I texted both of them, "We got a boss call and we're leaving in the morning. I will text you when I come back. Let's go out again!"

MATTHIEU

CHAPTER 24

When we reached St Thomas and I had signal again, a message from Matthieu pinged through. "Can't stop thinking about the other night. How was your trip?" I smiled and put the phone down to reply later when I could devote time to him. The flirty text conversations we had were a welcomed relief from the chaotic guest demands.

What seemed like years later, the boss trip finally ended and I messaged Matthieu to tell him the good news. "We're staying here for a couple of days and then heading back to St Martin. I can't wait!" "Maybe you don't tell Basem." Matthieu messaged. "We can just meet up alone if you like?" A huge smile swept across my face because I was most interested in Matthieu and would most certainly like to have him all to myself. I knew the threesome idea was a spontaneous not to happen again event, but I was happy to get between the sheets with Matthieu.

We reminisced about that crazy night in St Martin. "Would you really have had a threesome that morning?" I texted. "In that state of mind, yes probably. I've had a threesome with two girls, but not with another guy. I don't know. Now I wouldn't." I laughed. I must admit, that morning I would've gone crazy on the beach had people not interrupted us. However, it wasn't an experience I was interested in revisiting. At least not with those two guys.

CHAPTER 25

"I'm back!" I texted Matthieu after we tied up on the dock and had a celebratory beer. "Are you free this evening?" he replied. I was supposed to be on watch, but Grant told us we could all go out because he was tired and wanted to stay in. "So go out and get your rocks off guys." Grant is oh so charming! "Just don't visit Charlie this time!" he shouted sarcastically at me. "Yay!! I'm free now, so whenever you're ready, come get me." I texted Matthieu. "I will put some clothes on and go now." He replied. I practically ran to the gate to meet him.

Matthieu pulled into the marina and gave me a wave out the window. Wow, I had forgotten how stunning those eyes were. And that smile...the hooded lady was already hoping for some attention. I instantly melted at the sight of him. I was looking forward to feeling his soft sensual lips again and seeing what more he had to offer. After all, the French are supposed to be good lovers, right?

I shouted goodbye to the security guard and ran around to the passenger side. "Bonjour!" I smiled and leant over to give him a kiss on the cheek. "Bonjour," he smiled softly. He turned around and drove off towards the French side where his apartment was. "Are you hungry?" he asked. "Yes, always!" I replied. "Ok, I figure we go to my local pizza truck and take a pizza to my place. We can watch a movie. Sound good to you?" he asked in that sexy accent. Honestly, I would agree to anything he said because I'm not really listening to his words. His soft tone of voice gave him a mysterious air, accentuated by that gorgeous French accent. I loved watching his mouth as he spoke, imagining what his goatee would feel like as it caressed my clit.

We had a beer whilst we waited for the delicious smelling wood fire pizzas to bake. "There is not so much to do during the week here. I have to work tomorrow morning, so I don't want to go to the bar because it is always a party and I can't have just one drink," he said. "Are you ok to watch a movie?" "It sounds like heaven after the hectic boss trip I just had. I might fall asleep though." "Don't worry, I will give you a reason to wake up," he said. I raised an eyebrow and smiled. We were both on the same page. I relaxed even more anticipating the evening ending up exactly as I hoped. Back at his place, we ate our pizzas on his bed while watching French TV. I have to admit, it wasn't the most romantic of first dates.

"Do you want a massage?" Matthieu asked. "I would never say no to that!" I replied as I flopped over onto my stomach. If this is how French men treat their women, I was never going to date anyone else! "Ok, well take your shirt off first. I can't massage you through your shirt." As I took off my shirt and sports bra, he went into the bathroom to get some lotion. He straddled me and rubbed the cold lotion on my back. "Ahh! Cold!" I giggled. His hands were soft and gentle. My mind of course wandered to what else his hands could do... While the lotion chilled my back, my naughty thoughts created a warm moistness in my loins.

Not long after he started, I debated whether I should flip onto my back or not. I felt him move and looked up to see he was taking off his shirt. I set my head back down and smiled. I felt the heat of his chest get closer to my back. His soft lips gently kissed up and down my back. "Mmmm...." I moaned. I started to roll over onto my back, "Stop. The massage isn't over yet. Just wait." "Ok," I said obediently. His strong hands returned to my back. My muscles melted and my pussy became wetter. I reached back to grab his leg and see how high I could stroke his thigh. He moved my hand away and said, "Patience, sailor girl." He again kissed my upper back and I laid there subservient, enjoying every single sensual moment.

He slid one leg over me and kissed the side of my hip as he slipped my shorts and underwear down. He carefully tucked his hand under me and rolled me over to face him. He moved to the other side of me to kiss that side of my torso. He slowly made his way up towards my face. Stopping at my breasts, he gently rolled his tongue around my attentive nipple, while playfully squeezing the other. My chest arched towards him with pleasure. I couldn't get enough, I wanted all of him. His lips travelled to my neck and he gently started sucking, "Be careful!" I said as I gently pushed him away. "My neck is so sensitive and the last thing I need is to go back to the boat with hickies." "Hickey? What is this?" I laughed and explained what they are, "Ok, I will be gentle." His mouth made his way to mine and I parted my lips, ready to receive his tongue and melt even further into ecstasy. I was lost in his art of pleasure creation.

I yearned to feel his hardness inside of me, but the show he was creating for me was absolutely incredible and I wanted to revel in every sensual act. His lips sailed south again, teasing my nipples with his tongue, switching sides so they got equal attention.

Moans of pleasure poured from my mouth. He kissed my inner thighs and just as I thought he was going to lick my throbbing clit, his lips continued down towards my knee and then my foot. Normally I don't like when people touch my feet, but I was under a hypnosis of pleasure. He gently put my toe in and out of his mouth and I experienced a pleasure I had never felt before. It sent an electric current from my foot all the way up to my groin. I was under such a trance, that I couldn't even beg him to enter me, I just laid there, comatose with ecstasy.

He moved to my other foot, sending electric currents up that side of my body, kissing his way up once again to my inner thigh. His fingers gently rubbed my clit before entering my pussy. My head flew back as his tongue found my clit. This was taking foreplay to a whole new level. I grabbed his hair with my hands and let him lick his way until I orgasmed. It happened so quickly, I couldn't believe it. After a loud scream of pleasure, my body became jelly. I was breathing deeply and rapidly. He looked up at me and smiled, "Was that ok?" I laughed and wrapped my legs around him to draw his head up towards my mouth. "I don't know. You may have to try again," I teased.

Matthieu kissed me passionately and I felt his hardness pressing into me. I guided it into my still throbbing pussy, "Start slow until I'm fully recovered." The orgasm he gave me was intense and left my groin sensitive to touch and movement. It felt good to have him inside of me, "Ok." I said. He sat up and placed my legs on either side of his head. He wrapped his arms around my legs and gently kissed them as he thrust in and out slow and deep. He began thrusting faster and faster, squeezing my legs tighter to him. He closed his gorgeous eyes and tilted his head back with a look of pleasure on his face. He was lost in his rhythm, slowly building up to his own eruption. I grasped the bed sheets, my pussy still sensitive, but feeling as though I could orgasm again. My chest arched towards him as I took all of him inside of me.

After a few minutes, the rhythm of his thrusting changed, it became deeper and slower until he groaned with orgasm. He threw my legs to the side and flopped down next to me. He murmured something in French and grabbed me in his arms, kissing the top of my head. My pussy seemed to be throbbing to the beat of Matthieu's deep breaths.

We lay in silence for I don't know how long. I was lost in pure bliss and relived the gratification over and over in my head. I was amazed at how natural and comfortable it was for a first time. Matthieu placed his hand under my chin, lifted my head and gazed into my eyes. "You are so beautiful," he said before placing his mouth over mine.

His hands wandered over my still naked body and he pulled me on top of him. Although he was of slight build, he was very strong. I was still wet from what only seemed a few minutes ago. He was already hard and ready to start round two. I placed him inside of me and sat up. "Belle," he whispered through deep breaths. I grabbed his hands and placed them on my breasts, he gently squeezed them and rubbed his index finger over my nipples. They instantly stood to attention. I felt myself getting wetter and wetter. I slowed down to tease him. His hands came to my hips and he attempted to push them to his rhythm, but I smiled and pulled his hands away, "I'm in charge this time," I smiled coquettishly. "Uffff...oui!" He replied. I gently circled my hips around his cock until I began to orgasm. He felt my orgasm brewing, grabbed my hips and started thrusting faster and deeper. I came again. Just as I was about to tell him to give me a second to recover, his eyes rolled into the back of his head and his release followed mine.

I rested my torso on his, careful not to let him fall out of me. I placed my head on his chest and listened to his heart beating. He wrapped his arms around me and gave me a good squeeze. Eventually I rolled over to the side of him and nestled my head into his neck. "I suppose I should be getting back to the boat," I said. "Quel? No. You're staying here tonight." "I can't," I said as I pushed myself away from him. "The captain wants us to stay onboard unless we ask permission. Remember the last time we were together, I got in so much trouble!" "Oui. Five more minutes of cuddles and then I will drive you back."

On the drive to the marina, we discussed how we were going to handle the situation with Basem. "It was only the first night," I said. "We can wait and tell him after we hang out a few more times." Matthieu squeezed my knee and gave me that gorgeous smile. "I agree. You are so delicious, I think I'm falling in love with you." I rolled my eyes and smiled. The French really are the masters of love, even if it is bullshit.

CHAPTER 26

We stayed in St Martin for the next week, allowing time for Matthieu and I to continue exploring each other's bodies. Matthieu picked me up every evening I wasn't on watch and I became a part of his evening routine. During the week, we went to his place where he cooked dinner and chatted about our days over a bottle of wine. It felt like I had been dating him for years, but the sex continued to be fresh and new.

He was really funny and I quickly learned his sense of humour. I realised that a little twinkle appeared in his eye when he was about to tell a joke. Matthieu was so sweet and attentive in his love making. It was as if I was his blank canvas and he poured his love and attention into making the most beautiful masterpiece. After dinner, we cuddled together until the sexual tension became too thick and our bodies intertwined in throes of passion. We were having so much sex that it was impossible for me to be in a bad mood.

One evening, I noticed a little baggie of coke sitting on his fridge when I walked in. "Oh don't do that!!" I complained. "What?" he said looking around. "Why do you have coke lying there teasing me?" "It's a week day," he said, "we only do it on the weekend." "Maybe just one line??" I pleaded. He came up behind me and put his arms around me. Kissing my neck he softly whispered, "Aren't you a naughty girl." "Why yes I am," I said seductively. "Ok, just one," he said. After we each took a small line, Matthieu whispered, "Come. Follow me."

We walked to the bathroom and he turned on the shower. As we waited for the water to warm up, he started kissing me. He led me into the shower and without a word, he squirted soap into his hands and massaged me. Once the soap washed down my wet, glistening body, he crouched onto his knees and licked my pussy. I opened my legs wider to allow easier access. As I did so, he stuck two of his fingers inside of me. I thought my legs were going to give out from the electric sensation that shot up through my body. He had a talent for touching me in a way that left me begging for more. The speechless encounter elevated my arousal and all I wanted was for him to bend me over and fuck me hard.

I pulled him up to my face and grabbed the soap bottle. I returned the soap massage and paid extra attention to his hard cock. I knelt on the ground and took him in my mouth. I held him gently in my mouth as I flicked my tongue around the tip. He allowed me to play with him for a few minutes. I started off slow and gradually increased my speed as I squeezed my hand up and down his shaft. He pushed my head away from his cock. "Come," he finally spoke. He turned the water off and towelled me dry, occasionally giving me sweet kisses on the area he just towelled off. "Go wait on the bed," he said.

He ran into the room and jumped on top of me. "Now where we were? Oh yes, now I remember," and he flipped himself round so that his cock was in my face and his head in my pussy. The coke was heightening my pleasure and I couldn't hold him in my mouth. My hand stroked his member as moans of pleasure leaked from my mouth. Somehow, he was so acquainted with my body that he knew when I was about to orgasm, which I was quickly reaching. He made me feel like a sex goddess and the Colombian marching powder increased my confidence and arousal. He stopped and flipped me onto my back to suck on my nipples. The pleasure was unreal. "If all French men are like this, I'm not sleeping with anyone else," I whimpered. He laughed.

Matthieu bent my legs towards my face and started rimming me. I had only done this once before and wasn't sure how I felt about it, but as I completely trusted him, I relaxed and went with it. I focused on the tingling sensation shooting through my sex organs. I played with my clit, making slow small circles. I embraced the pleasure I was feeling from my bum to my clit. I moaned louder and louder and Matthieu lowered me down and fucked me. There was a gentle roughness to his actions that made me so horny and desperate to feel every inch of him. I flipped him over and sat on his hard throbbing cock. At this point, I didn't care about his pleasure, I just wanted to stay on the peak of orgasm for as long as I could. I alternated between grinding on him quickly and slowly, circling my hips to make sure he hit every single part of my insides. Eventually I couldn't take it anymore. I let go and pressed my hips down heavily to get him as deep as possible. I let out a huge scream as I orgasmed. I grabbed his waist to hold on. No way was I going to fall off this pleasure boat.

I flopped next to him, breathing heavily and unable to speak. He flipped me onto my stomach and entered me from behind. It was too much, my pussy was throbbing and I couldn't say anything. I couldn't tell him to stop, I couldn't move. I could only endure this heavenly pleasure. Within a couple of thrusts, he was finished and pulled out to come on my back. He laid next to my still panting body, "Fuck," he said. I turned my head to look at him, "Wow."

CHAPTER 27

I decided that motor yachts were not for me and handed in my notice. It was just in time as the Caribbean season was quickly coming to a close. I was desperate to complete my first Atlantic crossing on a sailboat. I focused all of my efforts on finding some sexy sailors to be "trapped" on the ocean with. I posted adverts on the relevant job forums and with only two days left on the motor yacht, I received a response inviting me to go for an interview.

The next day, Matthieu took me to the marina and waited for me while I spoke to the captain. The security guard checked me in at the gate and pointed to the boat that was on the end of a very long dock. As I got closer to the boat, I noticed a guy with shoulder length curly hair sitting on a table and staring in my direction. The closer I got to the boat, the more obvious it was that this long haired sailor was staring at me. "Ufff....here we go, we know what we have to do to get the job," I thought to myself.

I rolled my shoulders back and slowed down my walk, both to appear sexier and to prevent more beads of sweat forming on my brow and dripping down my neck. I put a smile on my face and pretended as if I hadn't noticed him. I approached the boat and I his jaw visually drop, "Hi, I'm Brizo. Tyson told me to come for an interview." After a prolonged pause, Gary gained his composure and stood up to meet me at the side. "Oh yes, of course. He just left, but he has his radio on him, so I'll give him a call. Jump aboard."

"Tyson, Tyson, this is Gary," I heard him call into the radio as he walked back to the cockpit. There were a bunch of girls working on deck. "Hi! I'm Brizo!" I introduced myself. They all said their names, which my nerves assured were quickly forgotten. "I don't know where he is. He just went to get a part, but he isn't answering the radio. I don't see what the fucking point of carrying a radio is if you don't answer it. Anyway, do you want something to drink while you wait?" "Sure, I'll have a water." "Still or sparkling?" the stewardess piped up. "Sparkling, thank you."

I placed my bag down on the cockpit table and stood out of the way of everyone working. I saw one of the other girls struggling to close and lock a hatch and I went over to her. "Can I help you?" Gary, being super attentive to me and my movements, noticed that I was talking to someone else and came up to us. "Oh yeah, this is a tricky one, you need a lot of weight on it to lock it. Here, let's all stand on it." It was a small hatch for all of us to stand on, so he got in the middle and put his arms around us. "Hey, can someone come over here and turn the key!" Gary hollered. Christina came up and locked the hatch. "Nice one team," Gary said after Christina managed to lock it." As I walked back to the cockpit, Tyson drove up alongside the boat in the tender. "Finally man," Gary shouted at him. "Brizo has been waiting for you." "That's alright," I replied. "Here, just take this Gary and I'll come up. Sorry Brizo." "Don't worry about it," I said.

Tyson climbed onboard and introduced himself. "I suppose you already met the rest of the crew?" "Yes, I did." He showed me around the boat, "We're just waiting for the chef to arrive and the weather is looking good to leave. She's coming the day after tomorrow and we'll sail off as soon as she's onboard. Is that ok with you?" "Yes, that's fine. It's my last day today." "Ok. Well you seem cool, so if you want to come with us, you have the position," Tyson said in a raspy Australian accent. "Yeah, I'm totally in," I replied. "Great. You can move in tonight if you want." "That's great. Thanks!" That was certainly the easiest job interview I ever had.

I jumped off the boat and practically ran back to Matthieu's car. "I got the job!!" I screeched. "Great," he said with a half smile. "When do you leave?" "The day after tomorrow," I said quietly. He grabbed my hand and said sadly, "Well then we have to make this a great night." He leant over and gave me a kiss. "But you come back?" he asked hopefully. The sailing lifestyle I had been living over the last couple of years hardened me to goodbyes. "I don't think so Matthieu. The sea has stolen my heart."

Matthieu picked me up later that evening for dinner. "I have a surprise for you," he said happily on the way to his flat. "Oh really? What's that?" "You'll have to wait and see," he teased. When we arrived at his house, he dangled a bag of cocaine in front of my face. "Tonight, we're going to have lots of fun so that you remember me and want to come back." "Oh no! That's such a bad idea, but I guess. I don't have to work tomorrow." "Sit down, what would you like to drink?" he asked me. "Ricard and water please. It's the last time I'll have a French guy making it for me," I joked. As he was pouring me a drink, he said, "Should we do a line now or wait until after dinner?" "Let's wait," I said. I knew that I would be interested in much more tantalising things than food after the white powder ran through my veins.

After dinner, we inhaled a line and laid down on the bed. I looked over at Matthieu. "Do you want to do a line off my pussy?" I asked. "I saw it in a movie and have been wanting to try it." His nimble body jumped out of bed so fast, "Yeah, for sure!" He reached for the cocaine, "Why you wait? Take your clothes off!" We both laughed and removed our clothing. He cut up the coke and very carefully transferred a line to my pubic bone. "This is crazy! I love it," he said as he rolled up a bank note. I tried not to laugh in case I moved too much and disturbed the adult candy. He snorted the line, licked off the residue from my skin and said, "Ok, now you do one off my dick?" "Ok!" I giggled.

"This is so crazy," he repeated in his irresistible French accent. I cut up a line and placed it on his semi erect cock. I turned my head and laughed. "Maybe someone should make a movie of us doing this and then we don't have to work," I said. "Don't make me laugh. Quick just do the line!" he said stifling a giggle. I inhaled the line, licked the remainder off of his dick and slid up his body to give him a kiss.

He rolled me on to my side and moved so we were facing each other. He began fingering me, increasing the speed as my juices become more abundant. The coke was sending my desire for him through the roof. I moved towards his waist, pushed him on his back and took his tool in my mouth. He was murmuring in French, which only increased my animalistic want for him. He tried to move from my grip, but I was in charge this time. I pushed him away and sat on top of him so that he could get a full view of me riding him. I felt as if I was in a porn movie and screamed louder and louder with each thrust, letting him know how much I was enjoying him. I fucked him hard and fast, the coke increasing our stamina. I tilted my pelvis back to bring my clit in contact with his body, stroking it as I rode him like a bucking bronco. He pinched my nipples hard and my pussy gushed with pleasure. "I'm coming," I screamed loudly. I braced myself on his chest, leant my head back, stuck my tits out and screamed. "Fuck yeah, oh keep going and fuck me hard," I screamed. He replied in French and my body erupted with pleasure.

"Get on your hands and knees right now and wait for me," he ordered. "I'm going to do a line of coke off your ass," he said. I did as I was told. "Wait, you are all sweaty, I have to dry you off," he laughed. "Whatever you say," I said to him breathless. He did a line, licked off the leftover powder and fucked me from behind. He entered with such force that I flew forward and had to regain my balance. He grabbed my hips and moved them back and forth onto his cock. I felt the blood rush between my legs once again. I wanted this to last forever. He left one hand on my hip and grabbed my hair with the other. The intensity of the passion made him rough and he was pulling my hair so hard it hurt, but I relaxed into the raw passion and didn't complain. He started groaning louder, muttering in French and then pulled out. I felt his warm oil ooze onto my back as he carried on muttering in French. I collapsed onto my stomach and waited for him to resurface.

As he laid on his stomach, I cut another line for myself and placed it on his bum. I snorted it and laid back down next to him. After we regrouped, Matthieu said, "What should we do now?" He picked up his phone. "It's 1 am!" he exclaimed. "Shit," I said, "The bars are closed now. Should we go to the strip club?" "Ok," Matthieu replied. We did a line for the road and Matthieu put the bag in his pocket. St Martin has a specific partygoer rhythm. After the bars close at 1, the crowds move to the strip clubs. When they close at 4 am, people either go home or if they're still coked up, move to the dance club where Matthieu, Basem and I began our story.

On the way to the strip club, I asked Matthieu, "Do they let couples get a lap dance?" "Yes, of course," he replied "Is any touching allowed?" "Depends on the girl, sometimes they let the girls touch them, but me, probably not." "Have you done it before with a girl?" I asked curiously. "Yes, once." "Should we give it a go?" I asked as I played with the hair around his ear. He looked at me with a sparkle in his eye, "If you want to, sure."

At the club, Matthieu was greeted by the bar staff and girls. He had been living in St Martin for the last year and was a regular at the strip club. The club was huge. The stage wove around the entire space in an S shape that ended with a bar on both ends. Sofas and lounge chairs dotted the rest of the space, creating areas for groups to sit and dancers to perform more intimate dances. We took two seats at the bar. Matthieu said, "Choose whatever girl you want." He started a conversation in French with his friend behind the bar while I perused the club. I saw a brunette dancer with a beautiful toned feminine body and large perky tits. I nudged Matthieu, "Look at that dancer over there with the brunette hair. What do you think?" "Sure.

Yes. This is for you as I probably will just be watching." "Let's get closer to the stage so I can put a dollar bill in her G-string." I stood up to move over and Matthieu ordered another drink, pointing to where I was walking.

We watched the dancer for a while as we sipped on our drinks. She was incredibly nimble and very sexy. I was getting excited and nervous about what was going to happen. I'd never had a private dance in a private room before. "You want another line first?" Matthieu asked. "Not in here, I don't like doing it in toilets," I replied, never taking my eyes off of her. "We go in the car then." Matthieu said. "Ok, let's go quickly!" I smiled at the dancer with a little wave as we walked past her and she gave me a wink.

When we returned, I couldn't find the dancer anymore. "Oh no! Where did she go?" "Don't worry. She probably went backstage to change before she walks around. Be patient." We sat at the bar and had another drink. "There she is," he said tapping my knee with his. "Should I ask her?" "Yes!" I said excitedly. He waved her over and my nerves increased. She was just as beautiful up close with her youthful, glistening skin. "Come. Follow me," she told us.

She asked the bouncer for the big room and pulled back the curtain. Mirrors covered the three walls. The only light came from a lampshade with giant holes covered with blue film to cast a soft and sexy glow. "I wait until next song," she said in broken English. "Where are you from?" I asked. "Russia," she smiled. "Am I allowed to touch you?" I asked her. "Yes, but he can not." "Ok," I said. Matthieu moved further away from me after she said this and I looked at him with a, "What's the matter?" expression. He smiled and turned away.

When the next song started, she moved her body in rhythm with the music. She gradually danced closer to me and placed one knee on either side of my thighs. She removed her lacey see through top,

Matthieu laughed and elbowed me. "Go on!" he mouthed. The cocaine must've started wearing off because I couldn't find the courage to touch her. I suddenly felt awkward and self-conscious. I put my hands on her waist as she grinded into me. She took my hands and put them on her breasts before playfully touching mine.

I looked over at Matthieu to find him laughing. I'm sure I looked so uncomfortable and awkward! She put her hands behind my shoulders and thrust her bouncing breasts into my face. I turned my head to look at Matthieu, who was wearing an entertaining look on his face. She leant down and kissed my neck, "Don't be afraid," she whispered. I giggled at how absurd I must look! "Can you dance on him?" I asked her. "Yes, but he can't touch. You can still touch me though," she shouted over the music.

The song was a long one and I was just starting to get into it. She grinded on Matthieu and arched her back so her head was in my crotch. She moved her head back and forth in between my increasingly warming groin. As soon as I fully embraced the erotic experiencing happening in my lap, the song changed. She climbed off of Matthieu, "Another one, yes?" she said. I didn't have any more cash on me, "Do you have any cash Matthieu?"

I asked him. He laughed, took my hand and said, "Come on. Let's go. One is good enough."

CHAPTER 28

We climbed in the car where Matthieu cut another line. "To the casino? Dominique and Ava are on their way there," he said. I really liked the two of them and Matthieu knew this. "Ok, but just for a little bit, I want to go home and be naked with you some more." I cooed. After all, it's not like we were sleeping anytime soon. It was already 4 am.

At the casino, Ava was mad that Dominique wanted to stay longer. She hadn't been drinking because she had to study for an exam the next day. I sat with her in the car park as the guys went in "for one quick game of blackjack." She became increasingly annoyed as time ticked on and they didn't come through the door. "Come on," she said. She stormed into the nearly empty casino and found Matthieu and Dominique at the slot machines with a full drink. Ava yelled something to Dominique in French and I went up behind Matthieu, putting my arms around him. As I kissed his neck I said, "Come on. Finish that drink and let's go back to yours." "In a minute. I want to finish and then play a different game." Ava ran off in anger. "You women," Dominique muttered.

Still standing behind Matthieu, I tried to help the situation brewing in my nether regions. I kissed him and rubbed his shoulders trying to convince him the activities at home would give him more of a thrill than the casino. Dominique said something in French and Matthieu replied in English, "She wants my cock," I spurted out a shocked laugh, then shrugged my shoulders and said, "Yeah, I do. Come on, let's go." After some more convincing, the guys eventually agreed to leave. Matthieu and I went back to his place. It was now 6.30 am and

I wanted to sit and enjoy the early morning sunshine on the beach in front of Matthieu's place. "I'm tired, let's just cuddle and sleep," he replied. I tried to initiate sex, but his interest left alongside the effects of the coke.

After a few hours of disturbed and restless sleep, Matthieu realised he wasn't going to get anymore sleep. He spooned me and reached around to play with me until I was juicy enough for him to enter. Contrary to the cocaine fuelled animalistic sex we had earlier that morning, the absence of the drug made for slow lazy mid-morning sex. We rinsed off together in the shower and he dropped me off on the stinkpot one last time.

That evening I moved on to the new boat and declined a dinner invitation from the new crew. I was so tired and I just wanted to stay on the boat and sleep. Matthieu had other ideas and insisted on picking me up. He invited me to watch his tennis match that night. It was my first and last chance to watch him run around the court, so I couldn't reject him. I watched him play his match. His focus on the ball and other player was the same as when he played with my body. It was hard to believe that less than 24 hours ago, we were high on coke, fucking like animals. Now I looked at him with desire, but I was physically too tired to do much about it.

After the match, we had some drinks with his friends. Most of them didn't speak any English and sadly the French language hadn't absorbed through my pussy. I found myself rudely nodding off while others were talking or trying to ask me questions. Matthieu, "Please can I just go back to your place for an hour and sleep. You can stay here and chat with your friends. I just can't stay awake." He refused, "I want to be with you. I will have one more drink and then we will go." I stood up and walked to the toilet in an attempt to wake myself up.

"Come on, let's go," Matthieu finally said. I think he was looking forward to one more night of sex adventures. I laid on his bed and the next thing I remember is registering the sound of the TV quietly playing in the background. I was still lying face down on the bed. "Morning sleepy," Matthieu said as he gave me a soft kiss on the forehead. "What time is it?" I asked groggily. "9.45." "SHIT!" I exclaimed. "I have to go, can you take me back please?" "Why you have to go? Just stay one more night here, you will be with them for a month." "I have no idea what's happening tomorrow and I'm new on the boat, so I don't want to come home too late. I didn't even get a chance to say anything more than hi to the captain because he was up the rig when I arrived today." Matthieu swooped me into his arms and held me tight, "I don't want you to go. You make my life so happy. I am lonely without you. I have nothing to do when you're gone."

At this point, I was so tired and exhausted from the last week of cramming in as much time as I could with him, that I couldn't even fake any empathy. I was beyond excited about my new journey and did not share his sadness. "When you visit France, let me know and I will come visit you. I will be back in St Martin next year, that's for sure." Without creating one last masterpiece of my body, Matthieu reluctantly drove me back to the boat. As I opened the door to leave, Matthieu grabbed my arm and started crying, "Please. Don't go." I honestly could not deal with it at this point. It took all my strength not to roll my eyes and say, "Get it together man!" I gave him a hug and smiled, "Don't worry, I'll send you a message when we get to the Azores. Time will go by fast." "Please don't go just yet," he pleaded. "I have to, I'm falling asleep and I have a long journey ahead of me." I got out of the car and turned back to blow him a kiss. This wasn't the first time I was leaving a lover for the sea, and I knew it wouldn't be my last.

TYSON

CHAPTER 29

We left St Martin and arrived in the Azores ten days later. When I got to the Azores, I turned on my phone and messages flooded through. Many of them were from Matthieu. I messaged him to say that we arrived safely. His usual immediate response did not occur and I assumed he was working. The next morning, I received a text saying he had met someone else and was happy. I laughed at the irony of how upset he was that I was leaving, yet ten days later he was already happy with someone else. With a mixture of relief and disappointment, I switched my phone back off. "Oh well, I'll be in a new port soon to find a new lover," I thought to myself.

As this was my first Atlantic crossing, my seasoned sailor friends filled me in on what generally happens. Upon arrival to the Azores, everyone goes out and gets obliterated. Normally the night ends in a crazy turn of events. If you're lucky, no one remembers what happened. After my alcohol and drug fest in St Martin, I was looking forward to going back to sobriety. The two years I had with Sebastian provided so much clarity and peace. I was disappointed in myself for breaking in St Martin and going back to my old ways. I told myself I wasn't going to have a drink even when we stopped in the Azores.

After we were securely on the dock and the boat was cleaned, we were set free. Some of the crew decided to take a nap, but Christina wanted to touch land and I was excited to explore the mystical Azores. It was a cold, grey, windy, cloudy day and it didn't take long before the rain set in. Christina took refuge in the shops while I waited for her in the doorway. "Ok, it's not so fun when it's raining. Should we just go to this bar and wait for the rain to stop?" Christina asked. I laughed, "Yeah, ok. I guess I can have one celebratory drink."

We went into the bar at the end of the high street. There was no doubt it was a local bar as everyone was speaking Portuguese. The barmaid didn't speak English, or maybe she just didn't want to admit that she did. The commentary and cheers of a football game on TV was the perfect ambience for the hazy smoke filled room.

We sat down and took off our wet jackets. We each ordered a beer. The bottles were tiny, so I thought one would be alright. I discovered that after 14 days at sea and an irregular sleep pattern, the body responds very differently to alcohol than usual. "Cheers," we said clinking our bottles together. "I've been wanting to chat to you more often, so I'm glad we have some time together alone to talk." Christina replied, "I know, I don't really get to talk to you, so this is nice. I feel like it's someone new after talking to the same people for the last two weeks," she laughed.

The first beer went down quickly. "Should we get another one?" Christina asked. "Sure, I don't even think this is half a pint. The bottles are so little and cute!" I said. She got up and went to the bar, bringing two more beers on her return. I tried to sip my beer slowly, but then Christina bought a packet of cigarettes and I decided to give up giving up smoking. After each drag, I took a sip and before I knew it, my beer was gone. "What time is it? " I asked. She looked at her watch, "It's 4 o'clock." She said, "Ok, so we have two hours before we meet the others," I replied. "Do you want another one?" "Yeah, why not," she laughed. I went up to the bar and ordered two more beers along with my own pack of cigarettes. I was past the point of return now. I knew I was in it for the long run.

"Oh shit, we're late!!" Christina exclaimed. "I hope you didn't want to go back to the boat to get ready," I laughed. Somehow two and a half hours, and who knows how many beers flew by in a heartbeat. It was dark outside and we walked along the seafront until we stumbled upon Pete's bar. Actually, we stumbled past it as we were so busy chatting away that we forgot to look where we were going. "Ok, act sober," I said to the swaying Christina. Or maybe I was swaying and she was standing still. Or maybe we were swaying in opposite directions. We both giggled and she said, "Ok. We got this!" We walked into the bar and Christina slurred over the loud murmur of voices and music, "Sorry we're late, we lost track of time!" The rest of the crew looked at us and said, "Where have you been?" Christina quickly slurred, "We were shopping." "What? For alcohol," sniggered Tyson. "Whatever, we had one beer," I said breaking my silence. "Yeah right!" Tyson laughed.

We sat down on opposite ends of the table disoriented that our intimate little world had been interrupted by a loud and busy environment. Someone ordered a round of shots and Tyson asked what I wanted to drink. "I can't do shots," I said. "Of course you can! You just need a chaser. What would you like?" "I better stick with beer," I replied with the most sober voice I could find. He went up to the bar and ordered a beer chaser for me. The shots and drinks came. It was tequila, uff! The terrible memories of times I overdosed on tequila came back with the smell. I nearly vomited in my mouth. I dumped a bunch of salt on my thumb to mask the taste and had a lemon at the ready. We toasted to a safe journey to the Azores and downed the shot. After a couple more rounds of shots and some more drinks, dinner finally arrived.

As the evening wore on, I was nominated designated cocaine finder because of my innocent smile. I didn't want to take any as I vowed that I had one slip up and wasn't going to have another. I resigned from the mission when one table I went up to said, "Be careful who you ask your candy for around here." Christina overheard me, "Oh, all you have to do is ask if they have any weed and if they say yes, then ask about cocaine. You have to go soft before you get hard," she educated me. I sniggered at her innocent innuendo. "Ok cool, you can ask then. I don't even want any." "Let's go outside and smoke and see if there's anyone to ask," she said.

We went outside and lit our cigarettes. We were the only ones out there leaving Christina's theory untested. Tyson came out the door. "Hey, do you guys mind if I join you?" He didn't smoke, but he was always puffing away on an e-cigarette. "Of course not," we chimed. Somehow the conversation turned to kissing girls. "I've never kissed a girl," Christina admitted. "What!??! You're 23 and you've never kissed a girl?!? At that age, I had probably kissed all of my girl friends," I confessed. "I don't know, it just isn't something we do," Christina said. "You have a lot to teach her," Tyson piped in. "You have to teach her the ropes of boats and apparently how to kiss girls." I laughed and then I reached over and grabbed Christina's head as I locked lips with hers. She easily accepted my tongue and I melted into it with the soft, gentle, feminine kiss. I pulled away and took a drag of my cigarette. I looked over at Tyson, who was stood there, looking at us with awe and his e-cigarette up to his mouth. "You alright?" I asked him. "I don't know if I saw what I just saw. Maybe you need to do it again." "Ok," chirped Christina. We kissed again while our captain, aka, boss observed. "This only happens in yachting!" I drunkenly thought to myself.

We were disturbed by some other bar patrons coming out for a cigarette. "Oh my word. I'm sailing across the ocean for the first time and I kissed a girl for the first time," exclaimed Christina. "So many firsts." "You're learning fast!" I chuckled. Christina finished her cigarette and went to talk to the people who had just come outside. Tyson looked at me with a cheeky grin, "I know I'm married, but that was really hot. I have something growing in my pants," I took one last drag of my cigarette, smiled, rolled my eyes and said, "You're old enough to be her father." I walked back inside with Tyson following at my footsteps.

During one of our cigarette breaks, Christina and I approached a lone guy about marijuana. He said that he did indeed know where we could get some. "That's great," said Christina. "Anything else to offer?" Christina asked innocently. "Nah, it's pretty hard to find anything else around here. With all the boats coming in, customs and the police are pretty strict. "Ah, ok," she responded with disappointment. "If you guys want to come with me, I can drop you off at the club where I'm going and I'll give it to you there." In our drunken stupor, we thought that was a great idea. "Club? Hell yeah?" said Christina wobbling from side to side.

We got in the car with our new friend and he gave us a little tour of the town. I was sitting in the back and despite it being freezing outside, I was starting to get the spins and needed some fresh air. He was whipping around the corners quickly, which wasn't helping my nausea. "Hey, is everything ok back there?" he asked. "Mmm..." I managed to mutter. Thankfully the club wasn't far away, so we stopped just as I was about to ask him to stop.

"You guys go inside and wait here. I'll be back with some pot," we clumsily clambered out of the car and went into the club. Christina loved techno music and dancing and she started jumping around. "Amazing music!" she shouted. The music was a good distraction from my nausea. We found a spot near the entrance to wait for our new friend and slowly sipped on our beer. I started swaying. I'm not sure if it was to the music or as a result of the copious amounts of alcohol my body was saturated in. I looked over at Christina who was spilling her drink as she rocked back and forth to the music. It prompted me to look down at my hand, which was also drenched with beer. "I think I've had enough to drink," I shouted into her ear. "Yeah, me too. I can't even stand up anymore!" she slurred. It felt like forever until our pot friend came back. "I need to go home," I mumbled to him. "Really? You haven't been here long." "I know, I just need to go home. I've been sober for the last 10 days and overdid it."

I barely remember getting out of the car and have no idea how I managed to get on the boat without falling in considering the boat was far off the dock and I normally have a fear of jumping on. I presume that Christina had to help me, after of course minutes of laughter. I remember telling Christina that I was going to go to the toilet. In my head, I knew that I was going straight to bed, but I couldn't yet admit defeat as Christina seemed to have sobered up after smoking. I went to the toilet, went to my bed and flopped face down.

The next morning, I woke up to the pull of the lines getting louder and louder and to my headache pounding stronger and stronger. I looked down and saw that I still had all of my clothes on. I tried to think long and hard about how I got home, but it wasn't coming to me. "Oh well, at least I came home alone and still have all of my clothes on." I changed my clothes and went to the saloon to see what the rest of the crew were doing. I could hear the chef downstairs banging around, so I went to see if she had a miracle cure for this killer hangover.

"Oh, it's you! Apparently, I am in a lesbian couple and you and Christina are together," Helga shouted at me. "Huh?" I asked confused. "And now I suppose you want me to make you some food after all of that. Well just so you know, I fucked a guy in a car last night, so it doesn't matter what you said." "What on earth are you talking about?" I said softly. "You told my fuck friend that I was a lesbian. You think that's funny?" "I don't remember Helga. It's probably something I would say," I muttered quietly. "Sorry if it upset you," She mumbled something in Slovakian under her breath and carried on making eggs.

The commotion aroused Christina and she came out of her cabin looking exactly how I felt, "Oh my god, I'm going to die," she moaned. "Me too," I agreed. "You girls are so stupid. Can't handle your drink. Why do you drink so much?" We both looked at each other and went upstairs. The crew had a love-fear relationship with Helga. We loved her food and all of the treats she made us, but she was often direct, abrupt and rude. "Come outside with me," Christina said. "Why? I just want to die?" I moaned. "Just come." I followed her outside and she promptly slapped me on the arm. "Ow! What the fuck?" I asked. "What happened to you last night?!? You left me alone! Do you have any idea what I've been through?" she asked half laughing, half in shock. "No. I had to pee and then the bed called me and I woke up face down, probably in the same position. I don't even remember coming on the boat." She started rambling about the turn of events that happened while I was in a drunken sleep.

"I sat on the sofa waiting for you to come back up and Tyson came up wearing only a long sleeve t-shirt and underwear and sat on the other side of the sofa. Not boxer shorts, but tightie whities and I was so freaked out," she spluttered. My jaw dropped open in shock. "I was going to go down to my cabin to get away from him, but when I looked outside, I saw Pippa and Richard coming back, so I thought oh yeah, they will save me," she continued.

"I sat on the sofa for a minute and they stayed outside, so I got up to talk to them. Pippa started taking off her jeans and Richard was being all pervy, grabbing her ass and kissing her. So I just went downstairs because it was the only place I felt safe!" she finished. "What?!?" I asked laughing as hard as my sore head would allow. "That is freaking hilarious!!" "It fucking wasn't! How could you abandon me?!? I couldn't believe it. It was so weird and now I really don't want to look at Tyson because whitie tighties are just gross," she laughed "I'm with you on that one," I chuckled. "It's cold, let's go inside now," she said.

We walked into the saloon laughing and not too long afterwards Tyson came up and sat on the sofa. Christina and I looked at each other and burst into laughter. "What's so funny? Did I miss something?" said Tyson with a look of pure confusion. "No, just the hangover giggles," I replied.

I opened my eyes the next day feeling fresher and with a clearer head. I heard the wind howling through the mast and rain pounding on the deck. I got dressed and went up to the saloon for Tyson's daily briefing. We were supposed to leave, but it was dark and super nasty outside. "I know the weather is shit, but if we plow through it for 12-24 hours, it will improve. We have a super tight deadline and we're already a little behind, so let's prepare the boat, Helga get any provisions you need and we'll leave after an early dinner." That was fine with me, I was happy to get back on the sea, even if it was windy and rough.

CHAPTER 30

Upon arrival in Mallorca, I quickly found work on another boat, but it wasn't going so well. I reached out to my limited contacts letting every know I was looking for work. Tyson was one of the first I contacted and he replied quickly. "I don't know of anything right now, but if I hear of anything, I'll let you know." "Great, thanks," I replied. "I have a feeling he's going to pull through for me!" I said to Lili, the super fun cook/stew I was working with.

We were eating dinner when my phone pinged and Tyson's name came up. "Oooo, he texted me already! Yay!" I said. I read the message to myself and looked over at her and winked. "He said that he's had too much wine tonight and has a confession to make." She looked at me with a sparkle in her eyes. "Oh really?" I texted him back, "Don't worry, your secret is safe with me." He quickly replied, "No, I shouldn't. It's the wine talking." I sent him an eye roll emoji and said, "Whatever. I'm not going to play games. If you want to tell me, tell me." I set my phone aside and Lili and I carried on talking. I saw my phone was exploding with messages, but I ignored it.

I climbed up onto the top bunk and opened up my phone. "Dios mio! You're not going to believe this," I said to Lili. "Digame? Que? Que?" Tell me, what? what?" Tyson said he noticed my tattoo when I went swimming in the middle of the Atlantic and he can't stop thinking about it. "I kind of fancy you," I read out to her. I have a monkey tattoo on my left hip which I got when I was 18 and started hating when I was 19. "QUE??" she exclaimed excitedly. "You went swimming in the middle of the ocean?" I threw my uniform shirt at her, "Shut up!" We both started laughing. "What are you going to do?" she asked. "He's fucking married. What a dick," I said.

But at the same time, I thought it's just words, no harm done. So... I decided to play the game. After all, we were in different parts of the ocean. I replied, "Oh really?" He came online instantly to read it, "Yeah. I want to have a conversation with your monkey." I rolled my eyes. Way too cheesy! "Not sure he feels the same," I replied. I turned my phone off and went to bed.

Over the next couple of months, Tyson sent me messages, often trying to engage me in sext talk. At first I resisted, but I had little else to do on the boat, so I started to answer his questions about sex positions and what I liked. Why not? It wasn't like I was ever going to have sex with the guy and it was entertaining. Plus, it gave something Lili and I to laugh about. He tried to convince me to send him photos, but that's where I draw the line.

I eventually left the job and was attending a yachtmaster course in England. During the written preparation, I got super flustered and needed help. I phoned Tyson in a tizzy asking for help. He told me to send him some photos of the chart and gave me some tips. "Thank you so much! It makes more sense now," I said gratefully. "Well, you can pay me in kind," Tyson replied. It was clear he wasn't going to give up! To be honest, he had started growing on me. I really liked his perverted sense of humour and his texts often sent me into a sexual fantasy wonderland. He seemed to know what a woman liked and there was something so sexy about that gruffy voice.

During my yachtmaster week, I started worrying about what my next move was going to be. I had already been invited on a romantic sailing trip with a guy I met in St Martin, but orgasms weren't going to pay my bills. At the end of the week, I received a message from Tyson. "Gary needs to leave for a family emergency and we still have guest trips. Can you come and take over for him?" "Perfect timing! Sure, that would be fun," I replied. I really liked the crew onboard and after crossing the Atlantic, the boat felt like my home.

Now I had a dilemma about how to handle Tyson. The text messages were fun, but even if he was single, I didn't find him that attractive. "You'll be sharing a cabin with me as that's where Gary sleeps. Or if you like, I can sleep above Thelma and Charlie and you can share with Christina." "I can be an adult and share with you," I said. My mind started wandering about different positions that would be possible in the limited bottom bunk. There's always the shower... "He's married," I reminded myself. There was still a week to strengthen my resolve.

PIERRE

CHAPTER 31

I lie on the saloon sofa, turned bed, waiting for Pierre to return after completing his pre-bed checks on deck. I'm still confused about what's happening, if anything. We had such a lovely day together. I arrived on the boat to a light lunch made by his niece. It was followed by a cheese and meat board, where I made the first faux pois, cutting the edge off of the cheese instead of eating it. The French are very particular about their cheese and he looked at me like I had murdered his cat! We motored out to anchor and had a lovely swim in a picturesque bay with the typical blue of the Mediterranean. I caught his nine year old niece making a heart shape with her hands behind my back. I thought it was so cute, but I'm not getting any sexual vibes from him. Now that we're alone, maybe I will be able to figure out what's going on.

Let me rewind to how we met. The motor yacht I worked on with Carl in St Martin was docked between two large beautiful sailing yachts. Sailing is where my heart is, so as I was cleaning clean things on the inside of the huge diesel sucking stinkpot, I glanced out of the black tinted windows to see what was happening in the world I really wanted to be in. One day, I noticed Pierre working away on deck. He was washing the boat shirtless, which showed off his perfectly sculpted abs, not too bulging biceps and broad strong shoulders. I paused and watched Pierre, noticing how his arm muscles flexed as he moved the brush back and forth over the deck. Mmmmm...it would feel great if I was feeling those muscles as his hands moved back and forth over my foredeck. In that moment, I knew I had to find a way to speak to him.

After I finished my work inside, I went on deck to see if Carl needed any help. Pierre was still outside and I felt the blood rushing towards my cheeks at the thought of us breathing the same air. "Hey Carl, do you need any help?" I asked. "Not really, but I'm sure the Frenchie over there does," he teased. Apparently, I wasn't as discreet with my glances as I thought was, or perhaps Carl was secure enough to appreciate the sheer beauty of this sea god with messy blonde hair and unkempt beard. I had yet to get close enough to see the colour of his eyes and gauge his height. "Fuck off Carl, jealousy isn't an attractive trait." We both laughed. "Alright, you can help me chamois. I guess you can take port side," he said pointing over to the side of the boat that was lying against Pierre's boat.

I started at the part of the boat closest to where Pierre was working. He looked up, "Hey," I smiled. "Hello, how are you?" he asked in a sexy French accent and gorgeous smile that lit up his eyes. I was already seeing Matthieu who introduced me to the pleasures of French loving. "Good," I said looking down shyly. "Your boat is beautiful," I said. Oh that smile. It was killing me! "Thank you. You should come over later and look at it closer." Oh my god, with that sexy heavy French accent, I would do anything he said. "Ok, thanks," I replied. I went back to work chamoising the stern and trying to keep my thoughts pure. I was failing miserably.

"Dinner is ready," Manuela, the chef announced to all of us. As we sat at the crew mess table eating, I asked Manuela, "Have you seen the hunk of a man on the sailing yacht next to us?" "No, I'm inside all of the fucking time feeding you fuckers," she barked. "Next time tell me when he's outside and I'll come look." "Yeah, what was with that? Are you going to fuck him?" asked Carl. I rolled my eyes, "Whatever Carl, I'm already seeing someone. It's just nice to have someone hot to look at while I'm working." "Anyway, he told me to stop by later so he can give me a tour of the boat," I added. "Make sure you get a thorough tour of his cabin," Carl joked.

After dinner, I sat out in the cockpit with Grant and waited to see if Pierre would appear. What felt like hours later, Pierre finally came out. He looked over and waved, "Hello!" I shouted. "Come over for a drink when you have time," he said. I stood up and said, "I have time now if that's ok." "Good, come aboard and I will get a beer." Grant just smiled and laughed at me. "Have fun," he whispered with a wink. "Whatever, I told you guys, I'm already seeing someone!" I practically ran off our passarelle before slowly prancing on to Pierre's boat. He came out carrying two beers just as I stepped onto the stern deck. "Welcome aboard," he said while handing me a beer. "Thanks," I smiled, looking into his handsome green eyes. He was much taller than me and his muscles bulged even more up close. "Let me show you around," he said. He led me inside and showed me the guest cabins and where he slept. He was sleeping in the master cabin while the owner wasn't onboard. It was hardly inviting as half of the bed contained a sail and his personal belongings. "I am leaving in a few days, so packing my things. It isn't usually such a mess," he said. Whatever, there was still enough room to be thrown on the bed and fucked deliciously with that perfectly sculpted body hovering over me.

We went back on deck and had a trying conversation. His understanding of English wasn't that good, I knew no French.

His broken English often made for an exchange of giggles while I tried to work out what he was saying. His stewardess climbed onboard, "Bonjour," she said. They had an exchange in French while I fantasised about him whispering French sweet nothings into my ear while our sweaty bodies moved to the waves of their own rhythm. He could just be reciting his to do list, but no doubt it would cause a waterfall of excitement between my thighs. "I need to get food for my crew. Do you want to come?" He asked. "Sure," I had already eaten, but if he was bringing food back, I may as well go along for the ride.

Pierre hadn't quite known how to communicate what he wanted to say. When he said, "I need to get food my crew," he meant, she already ate and let's get dinner together. In the car, he asked me if I liked sushi and it was then I suspected he had meant to invite me out for dinner. We went to the sushi restaurant which had a romantic ambience of low lighting, candles on each table and soft lounge music playing in the background. Pierre ordered a whole sushi platter to himself, while I ordered a spring roll. I was still full from the dinner I had eaten only an hour ago.

Throughout dinner, there were many awkward silences mixed with flirtatious giggles, while we tried to find out more about each other. His sexy smile put me at ease and when we couldn't make ourselves understood, we came to a mutual agreement to stop trying through a shoulder shrug and laugh. This was the first time I had ever been to dinner with someone where the language was such a barrier. I enjoyed being in his presence, probably due to the size and strength of his bicep muscles.

I felt guilty that my mind was wandering to naughty thoughts while I was dating Matthieu, but Pierre was leaving in a few days. I would rather save my energy for Matthieu who lived here. After dinner, we returned to the marina and said an awkward goodbye. Pierre gave me a hug and seemed like he was about to go in for a kiss, but I was a one man woman, so I quickly stepped back. "Thanks for dinner. No doubt I will see you tomorrow," I said. "There is dancing tomorrow, would you like to come with us? It is me and the stewardess and I think her friends." "I LOVE dancing, that would be great!" I exclaimed as I bounced towards my boat. I told Matthieu about the evening. He said, "Well I am a jealous person, but I guess you are not mine. You are a girl of the sea." I assured him, "Don't worry Matthieu, I like you and have no intention of seeing anyone else while I'm here."

CHAPTER 32

The next evening, I ate dinner in preparation for the dancing and then went outside to try and get Pierre's attention. He was sitting in the cockpit of his boat with his stewardess. He smiled at me and waved. I started walking off the boat and we met at the dock. "They don't want to go anymore. Would you still like to go with me? There is a nice restaurant next to the dancing where we eat." I laughed to myself since I had already eaten dinner again, but couldn't refuse his offer. After living for nearly two years on a sailboat with Sebastian, we often didn't have enough money to eat in the way that I was accustomed to, so I had lost a significant amount of weight. While the French men here in St Martin appeared to be falling at my feet and complimenting this slightly too slender frame, I wasn't feeling my healthiest. Having two dinners a couple of nights in a row probably wasn't a bad thing! "Sure, I'm really looking forward to dancing. I used to dance all of the time in Colombia and I miss it like crazy." We got in his car and drove to the other side of the island. "I'm sorry, but I have to drop something off at a friend's house. Is it ok? Then we go for dinner and dance," he said. "Sure, no problem. I don't mind having a tour of the island."

We arrived at his friend's house, who invited us in for a drink. They spoke amongst themselves in French, whilst I soaked up the luxury of their island home. The back garden was surrounded by palm trees and beautiful exotic flowers. We sat around a lighted pool that softly illuminated all of our faces. I was captivated by Pierre and his sexy graceful gestures as he chatted away in words I couldn't understand. I felt slightly guilty for having such strong sexual feelings for him when I knew Matthieu was jealous I was spending time with him. "I don't own you and you will be leaving me soon, but I am jealous of this man. Please don't fuck him," he said to me after I told him I was going dancing this evening.

At last, we finished our drinks and made our way to the restaurant. We were welcomed by a row of lit up palm trees and chilled lounge music inviting us in to relax and enjoy life. The maître'd led us to a table at the edge of the deck. I looked over the side and saw we were hanging over the sea. The music was playing softly enough that I could hear the roar of the waves crashing onto the shore. "This is beautiful," I smiled at Pierre. "Oh you like? Good!"

The waitress lit a candle that shined a soft glow on Pierre's chiselled chin. "You like white wine?" he asked me. "I love all kind of wine!" I responded. "Ok good, I will pick it out." He discussed the wine list with the waitress, who brought back a wine bucket filled with ice. The wine was delicious and I thought once the bottle was done, I was going to be needing that ice to cool myself off. This was turning into a beautiful romantic evening. Matthieu and I normally ate at his house in front of the TV as neither of us had the money for this sort of treat. Whilst I'm generally not a materialistic person, it had been years since I had been to a fancy romantic restaurant. I was soaking up the luxury of the ambience and the air of a captain who had enough money to treat me to an expensive bottle of wine.

Just as the night before, we had awkward and giggle filled conversations. This evening was more relaxed as we were comfortable enough with each other to say that something didn't make sense and to laugh at his English mistakes. His eyes twinkled in the candle light and I was not only disappointed that I was taken, but also that Pierre was leaving soon. I mean, who was I going to drool over while I completed my daily mundane cleaning tasks on the boat? The more wine we drank, the more relaxed we became and the more my mind was wandering to thoughts of his strong rough sailor hands caressing my soft sun kissed skin. I was deeply infatuated with this sea god whose language I could barely understand.

After dinner, we walked next door to a packed beach bar with five picnic tables lined up on a slant. The waves gently kissed the legs of the table nearest the shore. Fairy lights and candles surrounded the bar area and the salsa music was blasting. "Should we have a drink first before we dance?" Pierre asked. "Good idea, let me get the drinks," I said. I went up to the bar and ordered two beers while he sat down at the end of a picnic table filled with people.

I brought the beers over and we smiled at each other while listening to the conversation of those next to us. They tried to engage us in conversation, but we politely pulled away after one of the guests went into an alcohol fuelled rage over something insignificant.

We joined the other bodies that were enmeshed on the dance floor, twisting and gyrating their bodies together to the rhythm of the salsa, sweat dripping from their faces. We danced awkwardly at first, like two new lovers who have yet to discover the best way to satisfy each other's hunger. As our fingers found their place in between each other's, I immediately noticed how large and strong his hands were. I felt so safe, so feminine, so submissive. It didn't take long before I relaxed and allowed him to take the lead. He was a confident and strong dancer, which allowed my mind to drift off into thoughts of us dancing naked together, staring into each other's eyes as we create our own private dance.

After two songs, the music ended. "Shall we go back to the marina now?" Pierre asked. "Sure," I replied. We drove home attempting to discuss the angry guy that scared us off onto the dance floor. I noticed the time on the clock in the car 11.37. "Fuck, I didn't realise it was so late!!" I thought to myself. I told Matthieu that I would go to his place after dancing with Pierre and his friends. Matthieu didn't even know that Pierre and I had gone out alone. When we got back to the marina, Matthieu said, "Would you like to come for a drink?" Knowing I couldn't go, I decided to buy myself some time by saying, "Sure, I have to pee first. I'll be right there." I went inside and checked my phone. Matthieu had called and text asking where I was. I sent him a message. "Sorry, I didn't realise it was going to be so late, you can come get me now." He instantly came online, "Ok."

I ran outside to find Pierre sitting in his cockpit. I walked towards his yacht. "Do you want to watch the stars in the boom?" I literally stopped mid-step. "You can go in your boom?" "Yes, it is very big and comfortable," he teased. I had only been on small sailboats half the size of the one he was working on and I had no idea that was possible. I hesitated, knowing that Matthieu was on his way to pick me up, but really wanting to see the stars, but also not wanting to have to reject any advances that Pierre was clearly going to make. Being in my late 30's, I was wise enough to know that nice French wine and two romantic dinners would lead to an expectation that we would be doing much more than star gazing in that boom. I apologetically said, "Some friends of mine messaged to say they were going to pick me up for a party." I felt bad lying, but I didn't want to close all gates just yet. After all, one "friend" was picking me up to have a party in his pants... Pierre's shoulders fell and he said, "Ok. Maybe another time."

You can imagine my disappointment with having to reject sex in the boom with a strong, muscular and dreamy French captain! Although I could tell Pierre enjoyed spending time with me, he really hadn't tried to make any moves on me, so I was confused as to what he wanted from me anyway.

I saw Pierre the next morning as he was carrying his bags off the boat. I walked over to him and gave him a hug goodbye. "Maybe I will see you in France," he said. "I would like that!" I replied, thinking how that was unlikely to ever happen. Good thing I was wrong.

CHAPTER 33

Imagine my surprise when months later, a text popped up from Pierre, out of the blue, asking if I was free to help him sail his personal boat from Corsica to France. "I can do it by myself, but if there is two, it is more fun," he wrote. I was as single as a pringle and very much looking forward to picking up where we left off! This is how I found myself lying on his bed, staring at the deckhead wondering if the intentions of his boom invite were the same as his invitation to share the saloon bed together. He offered to clear out the bow cabin for me, but I was hoping to be wrapped in those burly sailor arms, so I told him it was unnecessary.

Satisfied the deck was secure for the evening, Pierre gracefully climbed down the companionway into the saloon and laid next to me. He wasn't close enough to be touching me, but I could feel the heat of his skin close to mine. I yearned for our bodies to touch. He was shirtless and I was wearing only a tank top and shorts, wishing I could take off the shorts and wrap my legs around his. It was a warm and humid August evening and the saloon didn't offer much for ventilation. I laid in a confused silence, waiting for him to move or speak.

"Do you have enough space?" he asked softly. Before I had time to answer, his big muscular arms swept underneath me and threw me on top of his warm, damp body. His lips found mine and we engaged in our first kiss. A kiss we waited four months to have. His tongue moved slowly around mine, while his hands crept up under my tiny vest top. An unconscious moan escaped from my throat.

He masterfully lowered my shorts using a combination of his hand and legs and kicked them off with his feet. His sailor strength rolled and slid us over, so that he was on top of me. His lips parted from mine and I moved my mouth back towards his, yearning for more. Instead, I welcomed his soft sweet lips on my neck as he gently pushed my head back. His hand caressed my body until he discovered the hot wetness between my legs. His finger was like a magnet to my clit and I felt my breath deepen as the blood rushed toward his finger, craving for more. I was so wet and so excited, desperate for him to enter me. His lips kissed their way to my nipple, where he gently started to nibble. He became aggressive in his bite and I instinctively wrapped my legs around him as I screamed out.

I found his mast and gently stroked it up and down. I pushed him off of me and gently nibbled on his ears before running my lips down to the base of his hard cock. I tease his tip with my tongue before taking the head of his cock deep into my throat. I'm slowly moving up and down his hardness, when he pulls me up and onto his chest. He starts kissing me deeply with his hand behind my head and his erection enters my dark wet tunnel. I sit up so I can watch his muscular chest and torso move along with the rhythm of my body. He places his hands on my tits and squeezes my nipples hard. Before I know it, I'm throwing my head back in pleasure as the juices release from my groin. Primal screams erupt from deep inside of me. After all, it had been three and a half long months since I had felt a man's touch. My shaking body and slower movements led him to flip me over on my back as he took over the show. He thrust in and out in an animalistic manner until he reached his peak and left his seed on my sweat soaked belly.

Breathless, he rolled off of me and our sweat soaked bodies laid next to each other. I turned to look at him and whispered, "Well that was totally unexpected, I didn't get that vibe from you at all!" He wrapped his arms around me and said, "I've been waiting to do that since the first night we met in St Martin." I rolled onto my side feeling satisfied and fell asleep with my vulva still swollen from the excitement.

CHAPTER 34

I woke up to a gentle caress on my hips. I'm confused. It's dark and I don't remember where I am. A strong hand gently reaches around me to tickle my clit as soft kisses caress the back of my neck. I smile as the memories come running back to me. I try to turn around and face him, but he holds me in place with those yummy sailor hooks. I reach back to raise his mast, only to find him rock hard and ready to go. The feel of his cock in my hand and the memory of what must've been a few hours ago, makes my pussy drip.

He pushes my upper body towards the wall and gently slides himself in. I'm slightly sore from the previous session, but my juices are flowing so easily that he slides in and out with ease. I lower my finger to my pleasure button and start touching myself, hoping to come before he does. I want him to feel my insides spasm with the pleasure he is giving me.
Mmmmm...lazy morning (or middle of the night) sex is the best. I grip my pillow. I can feel my whole body building up for an intense orgasm. He is deep inside of me, touching all of the right places. My feet clench and my back arches as my head reaches back towards him. I roar with ecstatic pleasure as my whole body releases into orgasm. The movement of my body must have excited him as just as I was finishing, he quickly pulled out and I felt a wet spot behind my back. We both fell back asleep without saying a word.

"Bonjour belle," Pierre whispers in my ear as he wraps his arm around me and pulls me close. He gives me sweet, soft kisses on my neck. "Shall we go swimming?" he asks. I laugh, "Great idea. Morning swims are the number one reason why I want to live on a boat." We're in France, there's no reason to put on a swimming costume. I float up the stairs and admire the beautiful view. I run towards the stern and jump into the refreshing water disturbing the serenity of the morning. I lie on my back with my breasts floating perkily, admiring the beautiful dawn sky. I feel like the luckiest girl on Earth. I may be unemployed with a dwindling savings account, but I get to live this life.

Pierre calls out to me, "We don't have much time. I want to eat breakfast and leave." I reluctantly swim towards the boat and climb up the ladder. After breakfast, we raise the sail and lift the anchor. We have a 30 hour sail ahead of us and I wanted it to be the slowest 30 hours of my life. Within the first hour, some dolphins made an appearance and followed us for miles. Pierre and I snuck flirty glances at each other. We had exhausted our limited mutual language and he was still trying to rig up an auto-pilot. I was hoping he would be successful soon so he could use his hands for other things. I sat next to him as he worked the tiller, making small movements. He gently caressed my inner thigh. "It's not fair to start what you can't finish," I said coyly. He laughed and replied, "Once I figure out how to make an auto pilot, we will see what happens."

Pierre and I took turns helming on the tiller. He finally found a way to jerry rig an autopilot as the wind became steady and strong, much like the fantasies that were playing in my head throughout the day. I couldn't wait for night to fall, not only because the sun was burning as intensely as my desires to feel Pierre enter me again. After the sun set, I went down to nap before my first evening watch. It took a while to fall asleep as images of me riding him the night before flashed through my mind. My sex organs were pulsing with excitement and I was tempted to run on deck and sit on his helm.

My alarm woke me up with a start. I grabbed a sweatshirt and went on deck. It was a beautiful clear night and we were far from shore, allowing the night sky to shower us in twinkles. I felt my insides warming and a dampness in my pants. "Hey. I'm really tired, I'm going to have a sleep before my next watch," Pierre said. The disappointment dried my insides as I smiled and said, "Ok. Sleep well." I had a hard time focusing on the tiller for the next couple of hours as confusion swirled through my head. Was he really tired or was he trying to avoid me? He went below without a kiss, without a caress or even a smile. This was our first time sailing together, so maybe I just had to get used to his sea rhythm.

Two hours later, a sleepy Pierre popped up through the hatch. "Hello," he said uninterested. I moved over so he could slide in near the tiller. He rigged up the autopilot again and looked over at me. "I'm sorry. I have to be honest with you," he said. My heart dropped into my stomach. He looked so serious, what happened? "My girlfriend broke up with me soon ago. I still love her and it feels wrong to have sex with you because maybe you like me," he explained in his best English. The smile quickly faded from my face and I was grateful there was no moon so he couldn't see the utter disappointment. "Ok, well, I never said I wanted a boyfriend. I just wanted to sail and it seemed like we had unfinished business from St Martin, so why not with you," I said.

Pierre placed his arm around me and pulled me into his muscular chest. He kissed the top of my head and squeezed me tight. "Ok, good," he said. My insides instantly reacted. I moved out from underneath his arm and knelt down on the deck. "What do you think you're doing?" he asked seductively. I looked up at him, "Shhhhh...." and gently removed his semi-erect cock from his board shorts. I moved my tongue from the base of his penis up towards the tip, which seemed to do the trick and he was nearly fully erect. I continued gently licking up and down until I felt him relax and harden. I tickled the tip of his penis with my tongue, while moving my hand up and down his pole. He moved his legs to brace himself against the other side of the cockpit. I wrapped my mouth around his cock and started sucking harder and faster until I tasted him in my mouth. I moved over to the side of the boat and spit over the side. As I turned around, he offered me his bottle of water. I smiled and said, "Thanks." He replied, "No. Thank you. That was amazing." I giggled and said, "I was trained well. A Captain is always supposed to get a blow job on his watch." I gave him a kiss on the cheek and went down in the saloon to nurse my disenchantment until sleep overcame me.

CHAPTER 35

As we got closer to our destination, Pierre made some phone calls. They were all in French, so I had no idea what was being discussed. He put his phone away and asked if I had ever heard of a supposedly well known club in Toulon. I replied that I hadn't. "Have you ever been to a sex club?" he asked. My eyes sparkled, "No, but I've always wanted to go to one! Is that what that place is?" He nodded his head with a dirty smile. I suddenly went from wanting to be on the water forever, to wishing the wind would blow stronger so we could get there quicker!

For the next hour, I questioned him on what happens at these sex clubs. He had been to numerous clubs, various times. "I just want to go and see what it's like because I've heard so much about them," I stated. He asked, "Do you want to have sex with other people?" I shrugged my shoulders and said, "Maybe if there's an attractive woman, I would be open to it. Maybe you and I can have sex while other people watch." A huge grin took over his face, "I think we will have fun."

We pulled up to the dock, where his friend was waiting to catch our lines. We went stern to into the berth and Pierre dropped the anchor off the bow as he backed in. He was taking a while to sort out the anchor so I went up front, "Do you need any help?" He smiled, "Yes, can you please get me the line that's in the stern." I fetched it and gave it to him. As he secured and tidied the bow, he turned around and suddenly screamed out in pain. I turned to see what was happening and he was standing on one foot shouting lots of expletives in French. I asked, "What happened?" and he shouted, "My foot, my foot, I think it's broken." Selfishly, my hopes of an evening filled with new sex adventures were instantly destroyed.

Pierre accepted my offer to help him walk back to the cockpit to sit down. He threw his long arm over my shoulder and leant on me as he hobbled to the stern. His friend examined the foot and said it was probably just a sprain. Pierre said it was way too painful and insisted it must be broken. "I want to go to the hospital and get an x-ray," he said angrily. His friend told him he had to go home and change cars, but he would be back to take him.

We were again alone on the boat, but with one of us damaged. I said, "If you go to the emergency room now, we could still make the sex club." He snorted in his French way, "They won't let me into the club with crutches. It is not happening. Every time I try to have a threesome something bad happens to me and it doesn't happen! Ufffff!!!!" I couldn't help but laugh and walked over to give him a kiss of sympathy.

"Come on, let's go inside now," he whispered to me. I bounced down the saloon stairs. "Can you grab the wood panels so I can close the door?" he said. Knowing there was only one reason why he would want privacy, I urgently handed them to him. He put them in place and laid down on the bed, "Well if I can't go to the sex club, we can make one here. I don't know how long I will be at the hospital."

I walked over to the bed, taking my clothes off along the way and straddled him. I bent towards him to take in the sweet taste of his lips, "Good, I love fucking you and we can always do it again after you come back." His tongue slipped into my mouth and his fingers found their way to my pussy. "Ooooo....I see you're ready," he replied with a shine in his eyes. I shimmied down and placed his growing hardness into my mouth. He moaned with pleasure and told me, "Take it slow so I don't come too soon. I want this to last. We have at least one hour before my friend comes back." After a few minutes, he pulled me up so he could kiss me passionately. I kissed his neck, "You're going to have to do all the work because I'm injured." We both laughed and I said, "My pleasure."

I grabbed his cock and slid it inside of me, careful not to let him go too deep too soon. I gently moved my hips back and forth with just the tip inside of me. His hands made their way to my waist and I said, "Not yet!" He murmured something in French as his hands found their way to my breasts. "Do you want me to go deeper?" I asked with a seductive smile. "Oui!" he shouted. I sat up and lowered myself further onto him. I slowly rocked my hips side to side getting him as deep as possible. He closed his eyes and moaned with pleasure. I brought his hands to my chest and told him to play with my nipples. He grabbed me and pulled me close to him, first kissing my lips and then teasing my nipples with his tongue. I gasped with pleasure and started moving my hips faster. Although he was in pain, he seemed to have forgotten his injury and moved his body in time with mine so that he could stay deep.

I was quickly reaching orgasm. I was so wet and so excited. I pulled myself away from him and said, "Stop for just a second, I'm close to coming and I don't want to yet." He laughed and said, "Well I can just make you come again." What men don't understand, is that the first orgasm never quite feels the same as the following ones, for me anyway. I wanted to savour the moment of being on the peak of orgasm. My mind shuts off, I'm no longer conscious of my body or how I look. I close my eyes and see a blurry blanket of stars as my senses heighten. A tingling sensation enters my groin as the wetness spreads and my thighs relax and open deeper. My back arches and my chest comes forward, nipples plump and erect. The only thing that disrupts this feeling is the orgasm ending. If a man is the right shape and/or experienced in how to touch me, this feeling can last for minutes. It isn't the orgasm itself that brings me the most titillation, it's the build up to it. I experience a heightened awareness of my pussy and feel as though I am the most beautiful and sexy woman alive. A man that can keep me there for long periods of time is a man that will always have a place between my sheets. Pierre wasn't this man, but damn, he felt good.

As I stopped moving my hips, he pulled me closer to him and sucked hard on my nipples. My pussy throbbed and the wetness increased. I gave up my playful resistance and scooted my hips so that his hard cock could once again dive into me. I sat up, moving up and down, putting my hands up over my head as I closed my eyes and lost myself in a moment of pure bliss. Ready to release, I placed my hands on his chest, allowing my pelvis to sink on his body. I allowed him to increase the rhythm. I threw my head back and screamed, "Oh yes! I'm coming, it feels so good!" His strong arms picked me up by the hips and threw me to the side as he moaned out in orgasm.

I cuddled up under his arm, neither of us caring about the heat or our sweat soaked bodies, he wrapped his arm around me and kissed me on the forehead. After a few minutes when we had caught our breath, he said, "Well I may not have gotten a threesome, but this definitely made up for it!"

The next morning, Pierre drove me to the train station where I was headed back to London until Tyson needed me on the boat. "I will call you when my foot is better and pay for your flight this time. Then we can go to that sex club," he winked. We had one last passionate kiss, his hand coming to the back of my head and messing my hair up. My pussy tingled in protest of having to leave him. "Heal quickly," I smiled as I got out of the car.

TYSON CONTINUED

CHAPTER 36

Back in London, I only had a few days to organise and store my belongings before flying to Itay. "Since we've talked so much about sex, what are your thoughts on it actually happening?" Tyson texted me. "Hmmm...well you're married and I don't really believe in being a mistress," I said. "Oh come on, we're sailors. I've spent two of the last 24 months with my wife, I have to get it from somewhere. Besides, it's been a loveless marriage for five years now. It's pretty much over." "Well when it's over, maybe I'll consider it." I replied. "We're going to be sharing a cabin, don't you think something is going to happen?" Tyson pushed. "I guess I am pretty irresistible," I replied cheekily. "Exactly and I'll be 50 in a few years, so it's time I have an early mid-life crisis with a younger woman," he sharply replied.

The night before I flew out, Tyson bluntly asked, "So are you going to kiss me when you arrive?" Man, he was persistent! "Hmmm... I don't know. I suppose we should because if it's bad, then we can forget anything else happening." I joked. "I'll take that as a yes, so just to let you know, I have a sun burn on my bottom lip that makes it a little sore. Be gentle and save the biting until it's fully healed," he wrote. "Noted," I replied. The truth is, I was hoping that something would happen. The little devil on my shoulder was speaking strongly and thinking it would be a great idea to be able to have sex while working. I felt like playing hard to get since Tyson was so keen.

I arrived in Italy where a driver was waiting to take me to the harbour where the boat was anchored. There was a guest change over and they were leaving the day I was arriving.

Tyson told me to wait in a cafe until all of the guests left the boat. The drive from the airport was beautiful. We drove through the dry countryside with terraces of olive trees dotted along the hills and mountains. Despite the air conditioning blasting, I could feel the heat searing through the black tinted windows. After spending a couple of days in England, it felt great to once again be roasting in the heat. We drove up over a hill and the driver stated, "Look over to your right and you will see the boat. She looks so beautiful in the bay." I looked over and a beautiful bay with turquoise water came into view. I saw the yacht boldly bobbing along in the water the colour of paradise.

We made our way over and down the hill, which brought us to the romantic little town. It was peppered with tired looking concrete houses. The pavements and some of the streets were cobblestoned and the striking bright purple and pink flowers added a nice accent to the sun kissed white of the buildings. We turned down one of the narrow cobblestoned streets and in front of me was a beautiful view of the bay. Butterflies started swirling around my tummy and I suddenly became really nervous. I still had an hour to wait until the guests left. The taxi asked me where I wanted to go and I told him to drop me off at the end of the dock so I could leave my bag there. I stood at the end of the dock admiring the beauty all around me. I texted Tyson, "I can see you!" and then walked over to the cafe where he told me to wait. It was a quiet little Italian town so I knew my bag would be safe for the next hour. My phone buzzed, "I can't wait for that kiss. I'll come alone!"

About 45 minutes later, I saw Tyson and Christina driving towards the doc. I ran over to them to say hello and gave Christina a big hug. As far as we were aware, the crew didn't know anything about our flirtations. I said "Hey," to Tyson and gave him a quick hug. "So we're just dropping the bags off now and the next trip will be the guests. Then I'll come meet you at the cafe." Christina and him started to load the bags into the taxi. My heart was fluttering and my labia started swelling, that voice was so sexy. It had been five months since we had seen each other and he wasn't as unattractive as I remembered. I watched his tall, slightly flabby figure move the bags from the tender to the dock. The sunlight gave his light brown hair a reddish glow. He flashed me a cheeky smile that reminded me of his mischievous personality.

I walked back to the cafe and tried to concentrate on the words of the book in front of me. My eyes kept wandering towards the boat, wishing for the time to pass quicker. After what seemed like hours, the tender full of people finally approached the dock. I paid my bill and slowly walked towards the dock. None of the guests knew who I was, so I thought it would be safe to pretend that I was some tourist just having a look at this beautiful super yacht.

I walked past the waiting taxi and sat on a bollard at the end of the dock. As the guests were hopping off the tender and saying their goodbyes to Tyson, I looked back impatiently. At last, the driver closed the sliding door with a beautiful bang. Before the car was out of sight, Tyson ran up to me, grabbed me and kissed me passionately. "Wow, I think the guests can still see you!" I giggled. "I don't fucking care, man I've had to control my cock since first seeing you. I tucked it up in my waistband. I forgot just how fucking gorgeous you are," he said as he grabbed the back of my head and pulled it towards him to give me another pussy stirring kiss.

"I told Christina there wasn't room in the tender so I could be alone. Do you mind if I get a coffee before we go back? I just need to get off the boat for a bit." "Not at all," I replied. "As long as you don't mind if I get a wine." "In that case, let's get a bottle and share. I don't need to be on the boat for any reason." "Sounds good to me!" I replied. Tyson ordered a bottle of rose and we chatted about his trip and the upcoming guest trip. He flashed a huge smile, "Damn you're so gorgeous. I'm so lucky I'm sharing a cabin with the most beautiful girl onboard." I blushed, "Thank you. You're very sweet."

We went back to the boat. He insisted that I sit next to him on the tender so he could run his hand up my thigh. Extended foreplay. It was only 4 pm and it would be hours before we would have some alone time. "Heeeeyyyyy!!!!" I screamed as we approached. I jumped up from my seat and bounced on to the boat as Tyson drove it alongside. The crew from the sister boat were also onboard enjoying their first evening off in ages. I screamed an excited hello to everyone and gave them a big hug and kiss. "Thank god you're here! Someone new for the boat!" They had guests onboard for 90 days straight and were exhausted and ready for a different dynamic. I couldn't blame them! Charlie grabbed my bag from Tyson and took it downstairs to the sex cabin. I soaked in how small it was. As I began unpacking my things, Tyson came in and closed the door. "I just have to show you something," he said. He came up and gave me another juicy kiss, sliding his hand up my shirt and moaning, "Oh my god, I want you so bad, I can't take it." "Patience Tyson, patience," I flirted back. He flung open the door and went back upstairs.

CHAPTER 37

After I settled in and donned my bikini, I went upstairs to join everyone who was already enjoying their celebratory drink. The bottle of wine that Tyson and I shared had already gone to my head. "What do you want to drink girl?" shouted Charlie over the music. "We have gin, vodka, tequila, wine, beer, fuck don't make me keep going, we have everything." I laughed, "I'll have a gin and sparkling water." "Do you want a lime in that? We got limes!" "Sure, why not?" I sat down on the bean bag and Thelma passed me my drink. Work started tomorrow, but today I was willing to be treated like a welcomed guest.

All of us girls were lounging on gigantic bean bags in the sunshine on the back of the boat. When it got hot, I rolled over the stern to swim until I was cool enough to once again bask in the glorious sun. Charlie was happy playing bartender, but he drank at a fast pace, so I was as well. Before I knew it, the sun was setting. It was a beautiful sunset. "I could definitely get used to this," I said. "Too bad we have guests coming onboard," I chuckled.

After sunset, I went down to the cabin to shower and get some warm clothes on. I left the cabin door unlocked, but locked the door to the head while I showered. I had a feeling Tyson would come in and I wasn't ready to give it up yet. I wanted him to wait. I washed all the salt off my silky body, dried off and wrapped the towel around my chest. I opened the door and sure enough, Tyson was there on his bed smoking his e-cigarette and scrolling through his phone. "Oh hello," he said coyishly. "Hello," I said with a raised eyebrow. "Something told me you would be waiting here. I didn't chamois as I knew that you hadn't showered yet, so sorry the floor is wet." "That's alright," he said as he got up from the bed, kissing me and slapping my bum as he went into the head. "Hey, I believe that's sexual harassment from the captain," I said with a wink and a smile. "Good thing I like it." "Ugghghh...oh my god, you," he said. Before he closed the door, I let the towel fall to expose one of my breasts, "Oops!" I exclaimed with surprise. "Argh! I can tell I'm going to be walking around with a permanent boner. I'm definitely going to have to wear underwear every day," he said shutting the door. "Oh, it's so easy to get men going," I thought to myself arrogantly.

I got dressed and went back up to join the party. I made myself another Monkey's gin drink and sat on the sofa. The cockpit was the best chill out area. The boat was very beamy so there was a sofa, two chairs and a coffee table on one side and on the other side there was a big dining table with a L shaped sofa and four chairs. As there was no other table other than the crew mess, it made dining al fresco mandatory. Charlie made a delicious dinner from the fish the guests didn't get a chance to eat and some roasted veggies. Quick and easy for him and delicious for us. We were all very happy and drunk at that point, so there was lots of laughter. Charlie was absolutely hilarious and great at making sexual innuendos and jokes.

After we cleared up dinner, we went back to lounging like the guests we so often serve. Christina and I were sharing a bean bag on the stern with the other girls. Tyson was in a chair on the other side of the cockpit. I had confided in Christina that Tyson was sending me racy messages, so she knew what was going on. She whispered in my ear, "Tyson hasn't taken his eyes off of you since dinner." "I know," I murmured back. "He's making it so obvious! Are you going to fuck him?" she asked. "I don't know, yeah, probably," I giggled. I was looking at Tyson the whole time I was whisper chatting with Christina. "What's so funny over there?" Tyson asked. "Nothing!" Christina shouted. "Wouldn't you like to know!" I winked. Charlie stood up from the bean bag next to us to make himself another drink. Tyson seized the opportunity to pinch his seat. "Oh shit, I need more wine," he complained. "Charlie, can you fill up my wine glass?" he asked. "How about you go fuck yourself. If you're going to steal my seat, you're not going to get anything from me," he said walking away from the bar with a cheeky grin.

As the night wore on, the music pumped, we were dancing as if no one was watching, and the alcohol was going down like water. Having worked weeks without a break, the crew started dropping like flies. I was riding high on adrenal and excitement and Tyson's cock was keeping him roused. On each side of the cockpit is a flat part where they put cushions for the guests to lie down. Tyson jumped up there and said, "Come here." He rested his back on the support and tapped his hands between his legs to indicate where he wanted me. I shimmied between his legs and rested against his chest. I allowed my head to rest on his shoulder and neck. He moved my hair away and started kissing behind my neck and ear. He wrapped his legs around mine and his arms around me and squeezed tight. "Hmmmm...I've been fantasising about cuddling you since May when we were on the crossing. I can't believe it's actually happening!" "Oh really? It does feel nice," I replied. I hadn't been dreaming of it since the crossing or even really at all, so I didn't have much to say to that. His touch felt good and his lips were so soft. I was so glad the sunburn on his lip seemed to have healed rather quickly.

We sat there in drunken silence, enjoying the sound of the waves lapping up against the hull. It didn't take long for his hands to start exploring the new territory. "Mmmm..." Tyson kept moaning. "You feel so good, you have such soft skin," he whispered.

He nibbled on my ear while unzipping my shorts. I wasn't going to resist or play hard to get. The romantic setting and the amount of alcohol in me made it easy to succumb to his touch. He gently slid his hand underneath my underwear and I unwrapped my legs from his to spread them for easier access. "You like that do you?" Tyson asked proudly. "Mmmm..." I moaned in response. He was teasing me gently with his finger, "Oh my god, you are so wet. I want to be inside of you." I reached my hand up and grabbed the back of his neck. "Not yet. I want to see what you got," I whispered. He carried on gently stroking my clit, every few strokes he slipped his finger down and inside of me, spreading my moistness for extra lubrication. My body responded intensely to his touch, my back arching to make it easy for him to kiss my neck and shoulders.

Tyson pulled his hand out from my underwear. "Let's get more comfortable." I got up and turned around, "No, you lie down," he instructed. I followed the captain's orders, sliding my shorts and underwear off as I moved. I kept them nearby in case the crew decided to come out for a smoke. Not like I would've had enough time to put them on, but in my drunken state, it made sense. Tyson grabbed my hips and slid me further up the cushion until I was in a half seated position. He gave me a few kisses on my neck and slid his head all the way down between my legs. His soft, gentle tongue made slow circles around my pink jewel, "Oh my god you taste so good," he moaned. "You FEEL so good," I said, "Wow." Any remaining tension left my body and my legs opened up yearning for more. I tilted my hips to help give him the best angle. He had a confidence and expertise like no other man who had touched me before.

He was in between my legs for what felt like 30 seconds and I was already about to come. Normally it's difficult for a new lover to make me orgasm with his mouth. "Stop," I said pushing his head way. "What's wrong?" he asked. "I'm about to come and I don't want to." "Why not? I can just make you come again and again and again and again," he said winking. "It's obvious you can, but the first orgasm is always the most intense and I want to savour this pleasure for a while," I said. "You certainly know a woman's body." "After 13 years of marriage, I hope so," he smirked. "Mmmm...yeah, don't remind me of that," I said covering my eyes. His response was to carry on with his oral expertise. The break helped curb the orgasm and I was ready to revel in the pleasure yet again.

A minute later I felt myself peaking again. Man this guy was good. I was trying to distract myself by thinking about work, but it wasn't working. I pushed his head away again and said, "Here, let me return the favour." "I don't want the crew to see their Captain's cock," he said. "Let's go up forward." "Ok." I hopped off the cushion and he grabbed me and turned to give me a sweet passionate kiss. Our tongues acted as if they had known each other their whole lives. He grabbed my hand, "Come." "Oh I will," I joked.

He led me to the bow of the boat. Up here we were free from the cameras and worries about the crew coming forward. Or at least we would see them first if they did. When I looked up, I was met with the beauty of a million shimmering stars. It was a clear night and the moon had yet to make an appearance. It felt like it was just the two of us in the middle of the ocean with our own private light show. Tyson laid down on the net and I straddled him. I unbuttoned his shorts while I admired the starry sky. I couldn't believe this was my life. How lucky was I to be on a millionaire's yacht in a beautiful bay, about to have what could possibly be the best sex of my life?

I took Tyson's shorts off and pulled his underwear down so that I could gently grab his already hard cock. "Someone's excited," I said to him. "Of course I am," he replied quickly. "I've been wanting to fuck you for months and you're so much more beautiful than I anticipated." I slowly moved my hand up and down his cock, pulling his foreskin all the way up and then gently all the way down. I bent down and tickled the tip with my tongue. "Oh god," he moaned. I liked how vocal he was, it was turning me on even more. I carried on tickling his tip as my hand became firmer around his cock, still going up and down slowly. His moaning became louder and his hips began to move up and down with me. I felt him getting harder and harder. I was dripping with excitement.

I took his underwear off and sat on his hardness. It was difficult to balance with the alcohol and the soft play of the net, so I rested my hands on his chest. He grabbed my wrists and tried to get deeper inside of me. "Just wait," I exclaimed. "I can tell this is going to be a great fuck and I want it to last as long as possible." Only the top of his hardness was inside of me. I circled my hips around his palpitating cock, his hands climbing up my arms and then back down to lift my shirt up. He placed his hands underneath and pulled my bra up so that he could squeeze my nipples. "Oh god," I said. Somehow, he knew the exact amount of pressure necessary for maximum stimulation. I felt my pussy getting wetter and I couldn't hold out any longer. I slid further down his cock, moaning with pleasure as I went. "Holy fuck, you are so wet, you feel so good," Tyson screamed as he squeezed my nipples harder. He took his hands out from under my shirt and grabbed my hips. He wanted to be in control of the rhythm. I resigned to the fact I was going to come very quickly. He pushed my hips down and moved them back and forth. I was screaming with pleasure, as was he. My knees were burning from the friction of the netting, but I wasn't going to let that stop my ecstasy.

Suddenly the guest hatch opened. I stopped, "Shit!" I whispered. "What's wrong?" asked Tyson. "Charlie and Thelma just opened their hatch." Tyson went up on his elbows and looked over. He laughed, "Oh well, guess the crew know we're sleeping together now." "Should we move?" I asked. "Nah, they already know." "Ok, I'll be quiet," I whispered. "I was just about to come too!" He grabbed my hips again and started thrusting them back and forth. He gently slid his thumb to my clit, still controlling the rhythm with his other hand. He didn't move his thumb, he just let the natural rhythm of our bodies do the work. I was peaking again. My rhythm slowed down, I closed my eyes, threw my head back and opened my mouth for a silent moan. I felt the orgasm rush through my entire body. My legs were tingling. I was out of breath and couldn't move.

The orgasm was so long and intense that it actually hurt. "Wow, I could feel that. That was so strong and it's still pulsing," he said quietly.

I laid my chest on his, "Just give me a second." "Fuck that was good," I said looking down to give him a kiss. He slowly thrusted deeper into me. I sat back up and reached my hands to his knees, thrusting my pelvis forward to get him as deep in as he could get. He grabbed my hips and thrusted quickly. His body jolted and he let out a not so quiet gasp. "Oh god!" he said. "Did you come?" I asked. "Yeah, sorry." "Next time you should ask your partner if she's on birth control." I said with slight irritation. "Oh shit, I just thought all women of your age are," he said. "You thought wrong." I gently sat up, letting the come drip down on him and laid next to him. "Touche," he laughed breathlessly. He put his arm around me and pulled me to his chest. "That was fucking amazing," he said kissing the top of my head. "Yeah, it was really fucking good," I agreed. We admired the stars while we caught our breath and decided that it was probably a good idea to get to bed as we had to work in the morning.

CHAPTER 38

The next morning, I heard Charlie banging pots and pans around the galley. "You go out first," I said. "I don't want to be the first one who has to deal with the shit we're going to get." "I'm the captain, I'm supposed to get coffee in bed before I go out," he teased. "Fuck you," I said sliding out of my top bunk and going to the head. I brushed my teeth and washed my face. Tyson was still in bed when I went out. "You're such a dick. Come on, please go out first?" "It'll be fine, don't worry," Tyson said with a smile. "Argh, I hate you!" I replied. I opened the door and Charlie turned around with a big grin, "Alright? Did you have a satisfying night? Of sleep that is?" "Yes, I did thanks," I replied innocently, walking through the galley and up the stairs as quickly as I could. I felt my face reddening with embarrassment. Not quick enough, "Yes, I heard," he said laughing. "Sorry!" I shouted behind me.

I went in the cockpit to see how I could help Christina and Thelma. They were sat at the table drinking tea. "Morning," they said in unison. Christina had a 'sooo...tell me' look on her face and Thelma just looked at me and laughed. "Good morning," I replied with my face turning a deeper shade of crimson. "Good night?" asked Thelma. "Yes, sorry," I said sheepishly. "What's going on?" asked Christina. "It was just a little noisy on the bow last night," Thelma laughed. "OH MY GOD! Did you?" shouted Christina. "Maybe," I said. We all started laughing. They tried to ask me more, but I remained silent. "Does he have a big dick?" asked Thelma. "He's your captain, I'm not going to say anything!" I chuckled.

Well, the secret was out. I was relieved as it's hard keeping secrets in a small space. It was going to be hard enough being professional around the guests. All I could think about was his hands running up and down my body. And that tongue.... It was only our first time and I was hooked.

The guests arrived that evening, so the mind blowing outdoor sex was put on hold for the next ten days. A couple of days later when I was helping Christina clean the cockpit, she pointed to my knees. "What did you do to your knees? Looks sore." I didn't need to look down, they were sore. "It's from the trampoline," I said humbly. She started laughing hysterically. "Oh my god that's going to scar and you're going to remember that forever," she said in between giggles. "I don't think I need a scar to remember that!" I smiled.

As the deck/engineer, I had one of the easier jobs onboard. There were only a few guests onboard and once the sun went down, my job was done. The culture onboard was to open a bottle of wine once the stewardesses were done serving the first course of dinner. Or with the case of Tyson and I, after sunset when we were finished.

Sometimes while the guests were eating, Tyson and I would sneak up to the bow and have our wine on the trampoline, keeping a professional distance just in case one of the guests made a surprise appearance. I enjoyed getting to know him. "I was gifted a boat about 10 years ago and my dream is to fix it up and sail around the world," he said. "My dream is to buy a boat that needs a lot of work, strip it down and then build it how I want it," I shared. "That's exactly what I have to do with my boat because it's been sat on the hard in Ireland for 10 years and not in such great shape." "Very cool," I said, putting the wine glass to my lips to hide my smile.

"So tell me about your marriage. What number girl am I?" I asked. "Well, we never see each other. In the last two years, I've spent two months with my wife and children and we're more friends than anything. She looks after the children and I bring home the money," he said. "You're the first girl that's sparked my interest, but I would say our marriage ended 5 years ago." "So why don't you let her go so she can find someone that would be around and appreciate her?" I challenged. "It's not that easy when you have kids," he excused.

We engaged in a long discussion about cheating, divorce and open relationships. "I wouldn't mind if my wife found someone else while I was away," he said. I couldn't help but laugh, "Oh really? Why? Is that because you've found other people and it would make you feel less guilty?" I didn't for one second believe that I was the first affair he had. He did it way too easily. He evaded the question, "We should probably get back inside and see if they need anything." I laughed and climbed in through the hatch of our cabin.

CHAPTER 39

Tyson and I did the tender runs together to make it easier to load and unload the children onboard or watch the tender if Tyson had to go somewhere with them. The guests asked to go to the beach every morning. One morning we dropped them off at the beach and Tyson said, "They're going to call soon as usual, so why don't we just float out here and have some alone time until they're ready." "Sure? Why not?" I replied.

He drove around the corner so we were out of view of both the boat and the beach. I sat on the seat just in front of the helm and Tyson put one hand on my shoulder and gave me a rub. It felt so good, there was something magic about his hands. It didn't matter if he was touching me sexually or casually, it just felt so damn good. He slowed down and looked behind him. "This should be good."

He turned off the engine and the only noise was the sound of the waves lapping against the rubber sides of the tender. "Go sit up in the bow," he said. "Why?" I asked. "Cause I want you to take your shorts and underwear off while I watch you masturbate from where you're sitting now." I smiled and got up, "That sounds like fun," I said. I took my shorts off and placed them on the seat to sit on. "Your underwear too, I want to see every part of you," he said puffing on his electronic cigarette.

I slid down my underwear and sat down. I placed my feet on either side of the inner tubes of the tender and looked at him. He was smiling and watching with anticipation. I spread my lips with my index and ring finger and circled my clit with my middle finger. "Like this?" I asked looking at him. "Yes, that's perfect," he said. I relaxed my upper body and felt my pussy getting wetter. I hadn't done this in front of someone I didn't know that well, but I could see from his groin that he was enjoying it, which in turn aroused me. "Are you going to do the same?" I asked. "Not yet, just keep going," he said. The warm sun on my naked lower half felt so good. I laid my head back on the inner tube and started moaning into it. I imagined fucking him on the seat where he was.

I felt the boat moving stronger and looked up to see Tyson coming towards me. He knelt down and started licking the sides of my pussy. I moved my finger so that he could take over. He gently sucked on my clit. "Take your shorts off and sit back down. I want to fuck you," I ordered. Without a word, he pulled his shorts around his ankles and I straddled him. He bit my breasts from the outside of my shirt as I guided him inside of me. This was no time for foreplay as there were boats around and we weren't sure when we were going to get a call to fetch the guests.

I grinded him hard and he put his finger on my clit. I felt him getting more excited as his movements became faster and faster. He squeezed my hips hard and kept my pussy pressed hard down on him. He gyrated his hips and closed his eyes. "Should I wait for you?" he asked. "Yes, I'm about to come." I wriggled on top of him, moving my finger quicker and quicker until at last my groin relaxed, my legs spread further and his cock sunk deeper into me. "Fuck yes, that felt so good!"

He didn't give me a chance to recover. He moved my hips up and down as he thrusted and within seconds, he lifted my hips up and came all over his stomach. "Let's go for a swim, I have to clean off," he chuckled. "Good idea," I said as I stripped off my remaining clothing. I jumped off the side. As I came back up to the surface, I heard a splash. I felt a little nip on my toe and Tyson pulled me close to him as he popped up. "Hello you," he said with a big smile. I wrapped my arms around him and gave him a big kiss before pulling away and dunking his head under the water.

I swam to the back of the tender and climbed up the ladder. Tyson followed closely behind and smacked my ass as I went up. We were lucky to have another ten glorious minutes basking our naked bodies in the beautiful sunshine before the guests called for a pick up.

Tyson threw on his clothes, easy to do when not wearing undergarments and he drove slowly as I collected all my pieces and put them on. "Fuck you're gorgeous," Tyson called over at me. I'd never really had a guy watch me so closely and be such a voyeur before. It was both flattering and arousing. "Thanks," I said flashing a shy smile. After I dressed, we drove full speed over to the beach and acted as if nothing happened.

Tyson and I had plenty of alone time to talk and get to know each other. I was going to stay on the boat for the delivery back to Spain, where Tyson would be reunited with his family. I kept my heart distant from Tyson, but enjoyed the attention and daily sex we snuck in.

One evening when the guests were eating dinner, I came into the cabin to take a shower. Tyson was lying on the bed scrolling on his phone. "I'll leave the door unlocked, just in case you need something from the head," I said. I went into the head and turned on the shower. Sure enough, a couple of minutes later, Tyson opened the door wearing only a big smile. "Hey, I thought maybe you needed help washing your back," he said. "Always," I said turning my back towards him. He came up behind me, gently patted my ass and kissed my neck as his hands reached around to cup my tits. I felt his baby beer belly press up against my back and his hardness press into my bum cheeks. "Oh sorry, I thought that was the soap," he said as he moved his hands away from my breasts. "That's ok, I already washed my back." "Well in that case," he said moving his hand down between my legs and sticking a finger inside of me. I have to be honest, shower and sea sex isn't my favourite, but so far everything with Tyson was amazing, so I rolled with it.

Tyson moved my hips back and gently pushed my shoulders down so I was bent over. He motioned for me to spread my legs by pressing his feet against my ankles, one at a time. Then he slowly slid himself inside of me. I turned the water off so that it didn't interfere with the natural lubrication that was happening.

He groaned quietly as he used my hips for leverage to thrust in and out of me. "Touch yourself," he said. I put my hand on the magic button and tilted my hips back so that he could go deeper inside of me. His thrusting became more aggressive, so I braced myself against the wall with my free hand. He squeezed my hips hard. I felt his nails digging into my skin and it was turning me on. I was getting wetter and swelling up with the faint hint of aggression. Before I got a chance to climax, Tyson let out a deep groan and pulled himself out of me. I felt his hot juice explode on my back. I stood up, "Now you can wash my back," I said turning the water back on. "You didn't come though," he said. "That's ok, you can lick my pussy later," I said looking deep into his eyes while casting a seductive look. He pulled my hair back and kissed my neck. "Fuck you're gorgeous. Where have you been all my life?" "Waiting for you obviously," I said sarcastically.

CHAPTER 40

At last! The guests left. Tyson let me pick up anchor and drive the boat to the bay where the sister boat was. When we arrived, we went swimming and then drank ourselves silly. Tyson said the chef deserved a break, so we got dressed up and went into town for some delicious authentic Italian pizza.

Tyson and I sat next to each other and he sneaked his hand onto my thigh. He leant over and whispered in my ear, "You look beautiful. I can't wait to take that dress off later." "For sure," I teased. "Since I'm not working, I pulled out the fancy underwear tonight." "Fuck, you're giving me a boner," he said wriggling in his seat. Charlie shouted across the table, "Hey you two, you already have a room, wait until you're in it!" The crew from the other boat looked over at us and the captain said in his thick French accent, "You two are fucking?" We all laughed and as neither of us confirmed or denied it, Charlie said, "Yep, they are! You should see Brizo's knees." "Fuck off Charlie," I giggled.

That night after everyone retired to their cabins, we went up to the flybridge to lie on the cushions and watch the stars. It was a beautiful night. "Tomorrow we should fill up the hot tub so we can sit in there and watch the stars," Tyson said. Another perk of working on superyachts, it's imperative to test the equipment to make sure it's working. "That would be romantic," I replied. I sat up and straddled him. I lifted up his shirt and tickled circles around his chest. He closed his eyes, "Hmmm...that feels really nice. You have such a nice touch," he said. "I think I'm falling in love with you," he said.

I stopped what I was doing and climbed off of him. "Don't talk like that, you're married and once you're back with your family, I'm not going to do this anymore. Just a bit of fun and games while you're working," I said. "Or maybe I'll leave her," he said. I laughed out loud. "Wow, if I had a dollar for every time a married man said that to his mistress, I would be rich!" "Now stop getting all soppy and decide where and how you're going to fuck me."

Tyson rolled over on top of me and pinned my hands behind my head. "Right here with me on top because you need to be punished." I wrapped my legs around him and pushed him towards me so I could reach his face for a kiss. His kisses were like the open button to my floodgates and a wet sticky patch formed in my black lacey underwear. He brought my hands together and held them with one hand. With his other hand, he swiftly took off his shorts, sliding them off with his feet. He lifted up my skirt and jerked my underwear to the side. He forced his way into my dark wet tunnel sending ripples of excitement through my body. Still holding on to my hands, he pulled my hair back with his other hand revealing my delicate neck. I submitted completely to his control, knowing he would sail me into a sea of sexual ecstasy.

"Fuck I love how wet you get," he said between thrusts. He was driving hard into me and the discomfort was surprisingly arousing. He pulled out, let go of my hands and kissed his way between my legs. He lifted up my hips and put his arms under my upper thighs. I started playing with his hair, but his hands somehow found mine and held on to them. When I tried to move them away, he murmured "Nuuhh, uh," the vibration of his tongue sent shivers up my spine and I stopped resisting.

His tongue was firm and focusing directly on my clit. Every once in a while, he stuck his tongue inside of my pussy and licked all the way back up to my clit. He was so good at going down on me. The pleasure sensations charged through me and in no time, I was at climax. "I'm about to come," I said. "Good. Let it go girl." I let go and squeezed his hands tighter, lifting my pelvis further towards his mouth and letting out a quiet scream. He quickly removed his tongue from my pleasure centre and kissed his way between my hips, up my stomach and stopping to bite on my nipples. "It's not over yet, I'm going to make sure you come again," he said.

Tyson sucked and licked my nipples, which were still standing to attention from the orgasm. I was like spaghetti in his hands. I loosely wrapped my legs around him and lifted my hands above my head to give him free reign to do whatever he wanted to my body.

After giving both nipples equal biting and sucking attention, he nibbled his way to my neck, pulled my hair back and looked into my eyes, "Ready for some more?" He was so attentive to how my body worked. We had only been having sex for a couple of weeks, but he knew when I was about to come, when I was coming and that he couldn't give me too much attention after my orgasm or it would be uncomfortable. "Yes, I am," I said pulling my head towards him for a kiss.

He pulled my hair back to deprive me of his lips. I was still juicy and wet so he easily slid inside of me once again. He drove deep and hard with long pauses between each in and out. "Are you going to come again?" he asked. "I don't think so, just fuck me hard or however you want." He plunged deeper and quicker and my hunger for him was insatiable. "Fuck me! Harder, harder," I begged. He lent closer to me to kiss my neck and bit my earlobe. His head drew back and he whispered, "I'm going to come. I'm going to come hard." He did his signature grunt and pulled out, jizzing all over my stomach. "Oh fuck, I'm so out of shape," he said rolling over onto his back, breathless. "I'm super dizzy. Fuck, that was so hot. You're so hot."

CHAPTER 41

The morning we left for Spain, Tyson confided in me that he was going to blame the weather for having to make various stops along the way. "I don't want to go back to family life quite yet." We shared the master cabin as our shenanigans were obviously no longer a secret. We did watches together and after one steamy session where we verbally teased each other the whole four hours, we had barely closed the door before stripping off our clothes.

Tyson threw me on the bed, "Lie on your back." I followed captain's orders and he put his tongue straight on my clit which was already wet and throbbing. He didn't spend too long there before his tongue trailed all the way up my abdomen to find my nipple, while his finger played with my clit. He sucked and gently nibbled on my nipples before using his tongue to find my pleasure button again. He repeated this sensual pattern over and over again, sometimes licking his way up to my mouth to give me a passionate kiss. Other times using only his finger while he watched me writhe in bliss.

"I've never experienced this before. It feels sooooo good," I whispered as my back arched in reaction to the glorious sensation. He was between my legs again, my hands gently playing with his hair and releasing as he went to tease my nipples. I was getting so close and as always, I never wanted that sensation to end. He stopped and went to go inside me. "No," I retorted. "I want to come like this. It's the best feeling in the world." He smiled and carried on. The engine was on, so when I was ready to release the pent up passion, I had no qualms about expressing the immense pleasure his act was giving me. We looked into each other's eyes as I peaked. He sat next to me watching me trying to catch my breath, "I think you liked that," he said smittenly. "I fucking loved it," I replied as I pulled his head in for a kiss.

At our final stop before Spain, Tyson fully turned on his romantic charm. He took me out for a seashore dinner just the two of us. He ordered fancy white Italian wine and fresh oysters. "I'm in love with you and want to leave my wife for you," Tyson smacked me with. My heart dropped as did my jaw. I was speechless.

"What do you say? Do you want to spend forever with me?" he continued. I sat in silence shocked at what he asked. "You do realise we don't really know each other," I said hoping to make him see sense. "I love everything about you, my marriage has been over for a long time. So will you?" Tyson persisted. "As romantic as that seems, I've only really known you for a month and I can't promise you forever." His face fell and he sat back in his chair. "I just told you I want to leave my wife for you," he said in angry disbelief. "I know, but I don't want you to." He huffed and the rest of the dinner was spent between awkward conversation and Tyson expressing his disbelief that I rejected him. I couldn't wait to get back onto the boat and to Spain.

When we arrived, Tyson offered me daywork and said I could sleep on the boat. "Tyson, that really isn't a good idea," I said. "You're with your family now and will be for the whole winter. Go try and make it work." He had a difficult time taking no for an answer. "How about this Tyson. If you decide to leave your wife, give me a call. Otherwise, give her as much attention as you're giving me." I packed my bags and left the boat. I was attracted to Tyson's sailing aspirations, his sense of humour and sexual prowess, but really all I wanted was a bit of fun

JEREMY

CHAPTER 42

A couple of weeks later, Tyson sent me a screen shot of a job advert for an Atlantic crossing from Northern France to the Caribbean. "I checked out his profile and he's super hot. Maybe you'll get lucky." I rolled my eyes as I ignored his unattractive jealousy. "Thanks."

I figured my chances of getting the job were slim because it had been advertised earlier in the day and no doubt there would've been a lot of interest. Out of curiosity, I looked up his Facebook profile. There was a photo of him and a woman from two years ago, but there didn't seem to be much since then. He looked young, had a big friendly smile and gorgeous curly longish hair. I sent off a witty email summarising my sailing experience, not holding out much hope.

A week went by and I had completely forgotten about the job post. An email from Jeremy, the relief captain, popped into my inbox asking me what time would be good for a phone interview. We arranged a time and had quite a long humorous conversation talking about our sailing experience and what the trip would entail. "Ok, well I'm just interviewing one other person and then I will make a decision within a day or two." "Ok great," I replied. The next day I got a phone call with the job offer. I was stoked! We were going to cross the infamous Bay of Biscay, which I had never sailed across before, so I was looking forward to the challenge.

When I arrived at the marina, we discovered that the gate was locked. "Ummm..so I can't find the gate fob, but are you ok to just slide your bag under the gate and climb over?" Jeremy asked. "Yeah, of course!" I said, passing him my bag. I climbed up and over and was in. "Awesome, you'll fit right in," he said in a heavy American accent. He asked about my journey as we walked to the boat. I noted he was much shorter than me, but very cute with gorgeous brown eyes.

It was late in the evening and I was exhausted from my 15 hour journey. Jeremy introduced me to the crew and briefly showed me around the boat. When we got to the master cabin, where he was staying for the crossing, I was amazed. It overlooked the bow and expanded almost the entire width of the yacht. The three external walls were all windows giving a king's view of the sea. The bed was massive and it had a huge wardrobe corridor leading to a luxurious head. He showed me to my cabin and said, "This door over here leads to the master cabin, but don't worry, the door is locked," he said with a nervous laugh. Although he was very cute, he was also very young and I had given up the puma lifestyle. Although I only had one year before I would be considered a cougar....

The next day, I woke up early and went into the galley where the chef, Seamus, was already working away. "What do you normally eat for breakfast?" he asked me. Sheila and Ron walked in, "Good morning," we all said to each other. I responded, "Normally I have my Tibetan medicine first, which looks like rabbit poo and then I either have yogurt and granola or eggs." Sheila started laughing, "Are you some kind of hippie or something?" "Exactly," I said with a big smile.

That conversation set the tone for the whole trip as every interaction we had together was full of laughter. That evening, we set sail with the intention to stop in Northern Spain and wait out some bad weather that was coming through. It took us about three days to cross the bay. The first night we had two people on a watch. I was the newbie onboard, so Jeremy wanted to make sure I was a competent sailor before we did solo watches.

We arrived in port at dusk having managed to dodge the bad weather. We arrived just in time because I was awoken in the middle of the night to the lines creaking from the stress of the wind and swell. The following day there were strong winds and it poured the whole day. It was hardly the weather to want to go exploring, so Jeremy declared it a work day.

I was anxious to go to the marina wall and watch the weather come in, so after we finished for the day, I asked if anyone wanted to come with. "Nah, I'm good," they all responded. "Ok boring people. See you later," I replied. As I started walking out, Jeremy had a change of heart. "Actually, I'll come with ya." I waited for him to wrap up in warm clothing. The wind was biting. It was November and we were in the north of Spain waiting out a BIG storm. The waves crashing up against the reinforcement wall that protected the marina were impressive.

Jeremy and I walked to the other side of the marina chatting along the way. We braced ourselves against the wind walking towards the wall, laughing about how difficult it was to walk. We were amazed that fishing boats were still crashing through the waves, business as usual. Jeremy and I lost ourselves in the storm occurring on the horizon. We barely talked, instead just observing the oncoming weather and making occasional comments about how we were glad to be in port.

After about half an hour, the cold wind against our faces became too much and we turned to leave. As we approached the marina bar, Jeremy said, "It's actually really nice getting off the boat. Do you want to stop and have a drink?" "Sure, good idea," I replied. He was a bit short for me, but he had beautiful longish crazy curly hair, gorgeous deep brown eyes and an award winning smile. However, I had just come out of a fling with Tyson, where I mixed business with pleasure and I wasn't keen to make that mistake again.

We opened the door to a blast of warm heat coming from the crackling fireplace. "Ahh, that's much better," Jeremy said. We ordered two glasses of wine and chose a seat near the fireplace. We were disappointed by the tiny amount that was in the glass, or maybe it only seemed small because the glass was half the size of our heads. We had one glass and decided it wasn't enough.

Jeremy was attentive and inquisitive. He asked about my life and listened intently. Tyson was more concerned about my vagina then my brain, so it was refreshing to have someone genuinely interested in what I said. "Where do you live normally?" asked Jeremy. "Ummmm....that's really hard to answer. Actually, I was living with my now ex and have been working on boats since then." "Oh, I'm sorry to hear that," he said touching my shoulder. "Thanks, it was actually a good thing, so I'm ok about it." "I not long ago broke up with my girlfriend," he admitted. "Was that a good thing?" I asked. "She was a really nice person, I just wasn't feeling it. You know what it's like. We both work on boats, so it's hard to see each other. And she was a lot older than me," he confessed. "Oh really?" I replied. "Yeah, she was 39," "Same age as me," I thought to myself.

My mind wandered to running my hands through those delicious curls.... Was him telling me his ex was an older woman, a sign that he was interested? I couldn't really tell. "Dinner should be ready soon, should we head back to the boat?" asked Jeremy. I was relieved to be interrupted from my thoughts that were quickly going south. "Sounds good, I'm hungry," I replied.

CHAPTER 43

"The weather isn't going to let up any time soon. We may be here for a while," Jeremy informed us the next morning. I didn't mind. I was in no rush to return as I didn't have another job to go to. Plus I kind of liked the area, despite the horrendous weather.

After work that day, we all walked to the marina wall to watch the waves that were even bigger than the day before. On the way back, the bar lured us in with the promise of warmth inside and out. Ron and Seamus had been victims of a wave and were soaking wet and cold. As more and more alcohol crept into our blood stream, we got sillier and our inhibitions loosened. All of us were smokers, so we took turns going out to smoke and ended up playing musical chairs. About three bottles of wine later, Jeremy and I ended up next to each other. The wine was making me outrageously flirtatious. From the conversation we had last night, I suspected Jeremy would be game to get his tip wet.

"What the hell?" said the alcohol devil. As we were listening to yet another hilarious story, I discreetly slid my hand under the table onto Jeremy's knee. He pushed his knee against mine and a few seconds later, his palm was on top of mine. His soft hand was the same size as mine and he gave my paw a gentle squeeze, sending an erotic jolt up my arm. I was still sober enough to care about getting caught in the act, so when Sheila looked our way, I quickly moved my hand off of his knee and onto mine. She gave me a weird confused look. Or was that in my imagination? She was quite bolshy, so if she saw something, I'm sure she would've made a comment.

I stood up to go to the toilet, "Are you going for a cigarette?" Jeremy asked. "Nah, I have to pee," I said. "Ok, I have to go too, do you want to smoke afterwards?" "Sure," I replied. He followed me to the bathroom and just as I was about to go into the ladies, Jeremy called my name, "Hey Brizo?" I turned around and he grabbed my arm and kissed me quickly on the lips sending a pleasant shock through me. He pulled away, "Wow. That was a nice surprise," I said with a smile.

He went into the bathroom and I paused a minute, pleasantly confused about what had just happened. His lips were soft, but it was a quick peck on the lips, so I couldn't really judge if he was a good kisser. I had an internal pep talk with myself in the bathroom mirror. "It's only 7 days into the crossing and you vowed never again to mix business with pleasure. If you're going to do something, at least wait until we're at the end of the trip," my well behaved side reasoned. "Oh whatever, he's young and hot and if he shows interest in you, go for it. It's only a temporary job, it's no big deal," the alcohol infused devil voice said.

As we puffed away outside, we came to a mutual agreement that if anything was going to happen, it would have to be in secret so the others didn't find out. Both of us were worried about looking unprofessional. This was the first time Jeremy crossed the Atlantic as acting captain, so he didn't want to jeopardise the opportunity.

Back inside the bar, we found it difficult to contain our lust for each other. Our feet found each other under the table and we snuck looks of desire to each other when we thought no one was looking. Waves of attraction and desire were flowing through my body. "Vale chicos, vamos! Estamos cerrando. Paga la cuenta y ya!" yelled the waitress. They were closing for the evening and kicking us out. We paid the bill and stumbled down the floating dock onto the boat.

I have an irrational fear of getting on boats and the wind had shifted so the boat was even further away from the dock. "Someone help me!" I screamed. They all turned and laughed, "You're going to have to learn one day," they laughed as they all jumped on casually and walked inside. "If I haven't yet learned in three years, can I do it another day please?" I pleaded. Jeremy took pity on me and came back to offer his soft hand. I grabbed it and jumped onboard, happy to get out of the biting wind and into the electric storm that was brewing between Jeremy and I.

"We're just going out for one more cigarette," Ron and Sheila said. Seamus had already gone to his cabin and Jeremy and I were standing in the saloon. "I've filled my lungs with enough cancer for the day," I stated. They walked outside and Jeremy waved me over to the door of his cabin.

There were three steps leading down to his cabin and he paused on the bottom step in the doorway. He pulled me close and gave me a passionate kiss. I giggled, "Not here, anyone could see!!" "Ok, I'll unlock the door to the VIP cabin and come in that way," he said. I felt a surging wet heat between my legs. Sex is a wonderful act, but it's even more exciting when it's 'forbidden.'

Without a word, I turned to go toward my cabin. Ron and Sheila walked inside as I was coming up the steps. Shelia gave me a confused look up and down and Ron stifled a smile. Too late, I saw it. "Fuck," I thought to myself. They already know. "It's too fucking windy out there," they replied breaking an awkward silence. "Good night, sleep tight!" I replied. I went into my cabin closing the door behind me. I waited five minutes before knocking on the adjoining door. I walked in giggling. Jeremy was waiting for me shirtless on the other side. "Welcome to my cabin!" he said with that irresistible smile.

I followed him up the steps to the bed. We both stood self-consciously next to it. There was some awkwardness that the amount of alcohol we had consumed was keeping under control. I started to have doubts about whether or not this was a good idea, so I wasn't going to make the first move.

Jeremy came closer and kissed me again. I became hyperaware of how I was taller than him and desperately wanted to be lying down. He must've read my mind because he led me to the mattress. Or more truthfully, I ungracefully fell back on the bed. He climbed on top of me and carried on kissing me. I have to say, I have been very lucky with good kissers in my love life. Or perhaps I just quickly run from the bad kissers. His kisses were soft, gentle and considerate. I was having a hard time relaxing and became very grateful to the alcohol gods for making this less unwieldy.

After what seemed like the longest kiss ever, I eventually made a move in fear that we would be making out until the early hours of the morning. I reached to undo his belt, which was as secure as a boat tied to the dock during stormy weather. He laughed, "Sorry. Even I have difficulty undoing this thing," he said as he undid it himself. While he was busy removing his trousers, I undid my jeans and threw them across the room. I moved myself up the bed so that my head was on the pillow. "Let's get under the covers, it's freezing," he said. We embraced under the covers, kissing and clumsily exploring each other's bodies. I felt like I was in high school again, having an inexperienced half clothed fumble.

I could tell that Ms Robinson, aka me, was going to have to make the moves, so I confidently pulled down his underwear and stroked his love piston. "I have to be honest, I may only last 30 seconds, so don't give me too much attention," he admitted. I giggled. "No problem. It's always best just to get the first time over and done with," I laughed.

His fingers crept underneath my panties and discovered a wet pool to lubricate his fingers. "Oh my god, I've never felt anyone this wet before. Wow!" I smiled and pulled them down to allow easier access. He drew his finger down from clit and gently inserted his finger inside of me. "Mmmm..."I moaned with pleasure. He clambered on top of me and I guided his piston inside of me. Just as I was starting to relax into the rhythm, he quickly pulled out. "Sorry, I said I was only going to last 30 seconds, " he said. I smiled and grabbed his strong muscular arms, "Don't worry. You're young, I'm sure your recovery time will make up for it."

We laid next to each other and I snuggled up to his chest, wrapping my free arm around him. He gave me a big squeeze and a kiss on the head. "I love cuddling. It's the best feeling ever," he remarked. "Well good thing we have that in common," I said as I wrapped my leg over his. I had yet to discover what his recovery time was like as the alcohol was now giving me a sleepy effect. Before I even realised, I had drifted off to dream land.

CHAPTER 44

"Good morning!" Jeremy whispered as the sun crept through the blinds. "Hey," I returned with a smile. "My head hurts so bad," I said. I sat up, my eyes frantically searching the massive cabin for my jeans. "I better get back to my cabin," I said. He rolled over onto his stomach and buried his face in his pillow. "Or you could just stay here and cuddle." I was tempted, but I could feel an impending hangover. I grabbed my clothes, gave him a kiss on the cheek and walked through the secret door to my cabin.

As I closed the door behind me, I ran my hands through my hair. What had I just done?!?! I grabbed my phone and texted my best friend, "I just slept with the captain!!!" I wrote. Her reply was quick, "Good on you girl! Tell me all about it, I love your stories!" with a laughing emoji. I pictured her laughing and wasn't yet ready to divulge the story.

I showered and got into some fresh clothes before going into the galley to make my Tibetan tea. The other three crew were already in the galley. Seamus greeted me with a cunning joke and everyone was reduced to laughter. "Oooohhh, don't. My head really hurts!!" "How about some bacon and eggs to clear away that hangover?" he said. "That sounds perfect." As I was eating, Jeremy walked into the galley, "Hey, hey everyone. Good morning," he said cheerily. "I just hate young people and their ability to be so fresh after a heavy night of drinking," Shelia replied. We all had a laugh. No one said anything about the two of us. I tried to avoid eye contact with Jeremy in case a glance was to give away our little secret.

With our sore heads, the only evening activity we could handle was watching a movie. Jeremy and I made separate beds on the floor while the others took their positions on the sofas. We each had a blanket over us and Jeremy placed his so that the edge of it was over mine. A table partially obscured our positions on the floor and Jeremy's cunning blanket placement further hid us.

Shortly into the movie, I felt his foot searching for mine. I slid mine closer and looked over at him. He smiled and held a finger up to his lips as if to say, "Shh.." I smiled and hooked my foot onto his, feeling a warm current run between us. I awoke to the lights turning on and movement in the saloon. I had obviously fallen asleep and missed pretty much all of the movie. We all said good night and went to our respective cabins. That day I resolved that sleeping with Jeremy was a one off. From now on we would carry on platonically, keeping our little secret.

CHAPTER 45

The next day I was more reserved and professional with Jeremy. I barely even looked at him. I was afraid those soul searching eyes and ravishing smile would send me running straight back to his cabin. I felt bad and vowed the next time we were alone, I would tell him I wanted to keep it professional.

That evening, I was in my cabin getting ready for bed when I heard a soft knock on the adjoining door. I walked over and opened the door. "Hey, I just wanted to ask if you're ok about what happened the other night." I smiled with reassurance, "Yes, of course. I just think maybe we should keep the sex out of it." "Ok, well I really enjoyed it, but I understand if you don't want to do it again," he said with a disappointed look in his eyes. "We can just cuddle if you want. We don't have to have sex again." "Thanks, but I'm really tired." "Ok," he replied. "Well, I'll leave the door unlocked so if you change your mind at any point, just come in. The invitation is always open."

"Thanks." I reached over and gave him a peck on the lips. "Sleep tight." I finished getting ready for bed and crawled into my own bed. I thought about his invitation and before I could change my mind, the queen of sleep had overcome me again.

I had to admit, I had a terrible sleep and I regretted not taking Jeremy up on his cuddle offer. My cabin was on the side lying against the dock and the noise from the lines and rubbing of the fenders startled me awake numerous times. The pouring rain motivated us to do nothing but watch movies after a short work day. Jeremy and I again set up our separate beds on the saloon floor and were bold enough to put the beds a little closer. Unbeknownst to the rest of the crew, we were holding hands under the blanket and Jeremy's sweet innocence was growing on me.

After the movie, we all said good night to each other. As I changed into my pyjamas, I heard Jeremy in his bathroom. I gently tapped on the door. He opened it with a big smile, "I really hoped you were going to come in tonight! I meant what I said about just cuddling." "Thanks," I went up the stairs and walked towards his bed. I turned around and walked back to the step. I ran and jumped onto his bed. I had been dreaming of doing that since the first day he showed me around. The bed was huge and I bounced up and back down.

Jeremy laughed. "Awesome, I can't believe I never thought of doing that!" He copied me, springing next to me. We pulled back the bed covers and curled up underneath the sheets. I lifted my head up and gave Jeremy a kiss. "We don't have to do anything you don't want to do, so I'll let you take the lead," he repeated again. He was so sweet. I nestled into his chest and quickly fell asleep.

In the middle of the night, there was a knock on the door. "Jeremy, wake up. I think a line snapped," Ron shouted. I quickly pulled the covers over my head. "Shit, shit, shit," I whispered. "Just a second! I'll be out in a minute," Jeremy yelled. He quickly got dressed and left me alone in the bed.

I wasn't sure if I should sneak back into my cabin or stay where I was. I decided to go back into my cabin just in case they needed more help and were to call me. Sure enough, there was a knock on my door and I called out sleepily, "Yeah?" "We need some help on the dock, can you get up?" Sheila asked. "Of course." I got dressed and went out to help. After we finished, I went back into my cabin, waited five minutes for everyone to settle and then snuck back through the secret door. "That was so close," we giggled. "Well, they'll probably find out sooner or later," he said. "I'm sure, but it's kind of fun having our own little secret right now." We snuggled back up in the middle of the monstrous bed and slept without incident until morning.

Jeremy finally gave us all a free day to explore. Jeremy, Sheila, Ron and I rented a car and drove along the coast looking for somewhere interesting to explore. We turned down a little path which looked as if it would get us closer to the shore. Wow, did it ever! "This is beautiful," I remarked. It was a grey cloudy day, but the foam of the waves smashing up against the dramatic rocky cliffs and dark storm clouds in the distance made for a visual delight. "You should find somewhere to pull over Ron," suggested Sheila. "Maybe we can find a way down to the beach, or at least get some photos from the cliffs."

Eventually we found a flat area off the path to park. We got out and walked down. Ron and Sheila were faffing about in the car, so Jeremy and I strolled off without them. It was an incredibly stunning view. The sound of the waves crashing onto the rocks provided the perfect ambience. Jeremy moved closer to me, "This is so romantic. I wish I could hold your hand," he whispered. "I know, that would be really nice." Sheila and Ron caught up to us and we all soaked in the beautiful scenery around us. "I'm so glad I'm not on the ocean right now," Sheila laughed. "Yeah, no shit. It wouldn't be so comfortable," Jeremy replied.

"I think there's a path down to the beach over here, come on, let's check it out," Ron exclaimed. We followed him down to the deserted beach with massive slabs of rocks scattered all around. "This rock looks like a big cock," said Jeremy. We all looked and started laughing. "It totally does!" I exclaimed. "Someone take a photo of me. I'm going to climb up top and sit on it."

Ron and I pulled out our phones eager to witness what hilarious show we were going to capture. Jeremy climbed on top of the rock and sat on the tallest point. Then he lifted his leg up and made a face like he was half in pain/half enjoying being tickled by the tip of a gigantic cock. We all laughed hysterically, Ron and I pressing away at our phones. "Ok, my turn," said Ron as Jeremy climbed off.

Ron put on a good show as he made different faces of pleasure, confusion and pain. My stomach was starting to hurt from so much laughter. Ron climbed down, "You girls want to have a go?" he asked. "No way," said Sheila, "but Brizo, you should have a go." I climbed up on the rock and tried to make as silly of a face as I could. I nearly fell off with laughter, so hopped off quickly. I was thinking of a different rock hard penis I wanted to climb later.

We continued walking towards a tall cave. Jeremy and I walked behind Ron and Sheila and he grabbed my hand. I looked over at him and smiled, "Really?" "Yeah. I was just thinking fuck it. I don't really care," he said. "We've been messing around for almost a week now and we're still doing our work. I'm not at work and I want to hold your hand, so I'm going to hold it." I squeezed his hand and we carried on walking. Sheila turned around and started to say something. When she saw us holding hands she said, "You guys are holding hands? What's going on?" We both shrugged our shoulders, "It's just so romantic here, why not?" Jeremy said nonchalantly. "Alright, whatever." Sheila must have been stunned into forgetfulness as she carried on walking without finishing her sentence.

After exploring the cave, we jumped back in the car and began a search for some food. We stumbled upon a little fishing village and stopped to walk around. The only restaurant opened had a stunning ocean view. We started the meal off with a bottle of red wine. As we toasted to a beautiful day of exploration, Sheila asked, "So what's going on with you two then?"

Neither of us spoke. We just looked at each other and then back at them. "Well clearly something is going because we saw you guys kissing that night we got hammered at the bar." She continued, "We aren't stupid. We've all been assuming that the door between the two cabins has been getting a lot of use." I laughed but remained silent. Captains are responsible in these situations. "Yeah, there's been something going on," Jeremy admitted. Ron laughed, "You have a thing for the older ladies, huh Jeremy?" He ran his fingers through those sexy curls, "Yeah, I guess." "Well as long as you two are happy, that's all that matters," Sheila said. I was relieved that it was out in the open, although I was a little disappointed the added excitement of sneaking around was gone. When we arrived back at the boat, Sheila announced to Seamus, "Well, they finally admitted what we already knew." "Great, happy for you guys!" Seamus said as he smacked Jeremy's bum.

CHAPTER 46

Alas, the bad weather broke and we were able to continue our journey. The next stop was a little fishing village in Portugal. Although this leg of the journey was only a couple of days, we had the traditional "we made it to land!" debauchery. We arrived at lunch time, so we peaked early and made our way back before dinner. Jeremy and I went into his cabin to warm up after a day of smoking at a table in the icy wind. Sheila went to bed and we could hear Ron and Seamus chatting away and laughing in the galley.

"Have you ever had sex in a boom?" I asked Jeremy. "No, have you?" "Nope, but I've always wanted to." The corners of his mouth curled up into a gorgeous smile, "Should we do it now?" I giggled and grabbed his hand. We snuck out of the cabin in hopes we wouldn't be discovered and ran up the fly bridge. We hopped on the hard bimini and crawled into the boom. We crawled/walked our way to the end where the sail was mostly flat and we could sink in comfortably. We sat there quietly for a second, "Do you think anyone can see us?" I asked as Jeremy came in for a kiss. "It's dark, does it really matter?" he said. He pulled me underneath him and gave me his signature body melting kisses.

Just as were getting ready to christen the boom, we both froze at the sound of male voices. We peered over the side of the boom and saw Ron and Seamus jumping off the boat. "Do you think they can hear us?" I said in a tipsy voice. "I don't know. I don't think so," said Jeremy. Apparently, I asked this question louder than I realised, "We can see your silhouette and we can definitely hear you," Seamus said loudly. Ron, ever the optimistic and positive soul said, "Good on you Jeremy, don't mind us. Just keep doing what you were doing!" "We're just checking out the stars!" I fibbed. "Is that what they call it these days, it's been so long..." muttered Seamus. They carried on down the dock and let us be.

"Now, where were we?" Jeremy asked kissing my neck. It was narrow and slightly awkward in the boom, so we each stripped off our own jeans. Jeremy laid back on top of me and continued giving me sweet kisses which provided a welcomed warmth from the icy cold air. I was more than ready to receive his sweetness, so I guided him into me as he wriggled his legs to try and get a comfortable position.

I looked up to enjoy the view. Despite the lights of the marina, I could see the beautiful twinkle of a starlit night. "Does it get any more romantic than this??" I thought to myself. "Hold on, I feel something hard on my knee which kinda hurts," Jeremy interrupted. "I feel something hard too, but I like it" I joked. He tried to arrange himself to get comfortable, but it didn't seem to be working. In fear that he would lose the rock hard erection I was enjoying inside of me, I said, "Let's switch positions." We clumsily fumbled so that Jeremy was on the bottom while I straddled him. It was a good thing neither of us were big people because my knees were smashed up against the side.

I tried to find a good rhythm, but the lack of a range of motion and the stiff, hard stitching of the sail made it difficult to relax and enjoy this new and what was supposed to be exciting experience I had been dreaming of. "The stars are amazing," whispered Jeremy. I was relieved to have an excuse from the stiff sail rubbing on my knees. I looked up. "I know. There's 'O-Ryan's' belt. It's my new favourite constellation."

We were once again interrupted by the murmur of male voices. I looked over to the side and saw Ron and Seamus returning from whatever mission they had been on. "They're back," I said climbing off Jeremy. I squeezed into the narrow space beside Jeremy. "Hey Brizo. Is Jeremy still up there? I saw you sitting up, but what happened to Jeremy?" "He's a little busy up here right now," I shouted down. "Hey buddy! You ok up there?" Ron joked. "Should we send up some help?" "Thanks guys, I'm alright," Jeremy barked back.

CHAPTER 47

The next leg brought us to the Southern most part of the journey before we tacked west to the Caribbean. I had never been to the Cape Verde islands and was excited about seeing a new place. Large brown/black mountains amongst a clear blue sky loomed ahead of us.

I grabbed the binoculars and explored the land through magnified eyes. They were met with barren land. Dark soil, volcanic rock and leafless trees randomly scattered the hillsides. The sun warmed up the black soil and the onshore breeze delivered a wave of hot air over us. Tiny little colourful shacks began to appear as we entered the bay. Fishermen in beat up old wooden boats sped out beside us to ask us if we had any trash to get rid of, or if we wanted any fish. A big yacht signifies big cash to them. It was a race to see who could earn the income first. Jeremy radioed the marina and the usual excitement of discovering a new land ran through my veins. I had no idea what to expect from this island, it was all new to me.

That evening we all went out for dinner in Mindelo. There weren't many options to choose from, so we chose the busiest restaurant and asked for a table of five. We ordered gins and rums and they came out with the bottles of hard liquor and glasses filled with ice. The waiter placed the mixers in front of us and poured gin in my glass. It was a large glass and he kept going and going. I only really took notice when Ron said, "Alright mate, that's enough." There was only a couple of centimetres left for my sparkling water mixer. I started laughing hysterically, "Well they certainly are generous with their pour here!" I remarked. Ron laughed and said, "I think they pour until we say stop." "Oops! I don't think I'll need another one to get it right the next time."

We had a delicious seafood dinner and stayed for some more drinks. The town centre was much livelier on the way back to the marina. Latin American music played loudly in the square with couples of all ages dancing the night away. We all stopped to watch for a while. "Do you like to dance?" I turned and asked Jeremy. "I love to dance, come on!" He grabbed my hand and we walked towards the centre of the square to show the locals our moves. I tend not to trust new dance partners, so I was having a hard time following him. I kept letting go of his hand when he wanted to spin me and stepped on his feet a couple of times. It was as awkward and comical as the first time we had sex.

We put serious looks on our faces and pretended we fit right in with the much more talented locals around us. "Do you think they're laughing at us?" Jeremy asked. "Probably. Or they're just jealous they don't look as good as us," I teased. "Alright, let's give them a show."

Jeremy let go of my hand and started dancing his way to the edge of the square. I stayed where I was and did a little solo dance looking at him while trying not to laugh. Jeremy danced his way back towards me, making little salsa steps and rolling his hands in circles around each other, I held my arms out and started shaking my tatas at him. From the corner of my eye, I caught the locals pointing at us, hooting with laughter. We looked at each other and giggled. We quickly regained our composure and reached our arms out to each other, beckoning the other closer with our index fingers. We sexily gazed into each other's eyes and then passed each other without touching or dancing together.

I laughed and turned around. Jeremy turned around and we danced towards each other again. This time he grabbed my hand, spun me around and we carried on pretending to be professional salsa dancers. "I think we've shown them enough of how white people can't dance, what do you think?" asked Jeremy. "Yep!" I replied. We danced our way out of the square in fits of giggles. The crew applauded us. "It's like you were meant for each other," Sheila roared. "You don't mind if you look like total twats in front of strangers."

Back on the boat, we quickly said our good nights and ran off to our abode of love. The air had been hot and humid, leaving us wet and sticky. We went into the shower together. Jeremy was known for his two minute showers, so I encouraged him to stay longer by giving him a sensual massage as I soaped up his body. As I washed his back, I reached around him and stroked his cock up and down slowly. I gave him soft gentle kisses on his neck and behind his ear. He moaned softly. "I've never had such great service in a shower before," he said. "At your service," I teased.

I stepped out of the shower and wrapped a towel underneath my armpits before meandering to the bed. Jeremy followed. I threw my towel off before getting underneath the covers. "Ooooo...I want to get closer to that!" he said. He jumped into bed and laid on top of me. His solid chest felt cool against my naked breasts. He turned his head and placed his mouth over mine giving me a deep passionate kiss.

"How do you want to be loved tonight?" he asked. "Rough," I said mischievously. "What? Like choking you? Getting tied up? Whipped? Spanked?" he asked. We both started laughing. "I guess this is new for you, huh?" I asked. "Maybe," he said stuffing my nipple into his mouth. "Ok, let's start by you tying me up. This is the perfect bed for it," I said. "I don't have any rope in here," he replied. I looked at him and shrugged my shoulders. "Ok, fine!" he groaned. He put on his pyjama shorts and went out to find some loose bits of rope.

Jeremy burst through the door with an authoritative attitude. "Put your hands up over your head," he ordered. "Yes Captain," I said with a sexy smile. He tied my hands on either side of the bed. "See if you can get out of that!" he challenged. I moved my hands and the knots got tighter. "Nope, I can't." I lifted my head to try and give him a kiss and he rejected me. He licked my neck all the way down to my pussy. He spread my legs further apart.

"Good thing I brought lots of rope," he said. He tied my legs up so I was in a star position. "This is going to be fun!" I said. "Who knows, I'm just making this shit up," he laughed. His tongue played with my rosebud, the restriction of movement enhancing my pleasure. I was writhing around the bed, desperate to find a way to touch him somehow. "No moving," he shouted. "I can't help it, you're super talented with your tongue," I protested. While he licked me up and down faster and faster, he stuck his fingers inside of me and slowly went in and out making me wetter and wetter. My legs tensed, my toes curled and I gave a quiet moan of pleasure as the sea moved below me. The intensity of pleasure left me feeling weak and vulnerable.

"Oh my god, that was so good," I said. "Shut up and listen to what I tell you to do," he demanded. Oh good, it wasn't over! He untied my feet first, "Don't move until I say," and then my hands. "Roll over on your stomach and get on your knees," he said. "Anything you say Captain," I replied submissively.

He tied my hands together and I rested on my forearms with my hips and bum in the air. "You want to do anal?" he asked me. "If you have a way to lube me up, sure," I replied. "Fuck," he said. "We need to hit up a pharmacy ASAP," he said. Instead, he grabbed my hips and pushed himself hard inside of me. He thrusted hard and fast and smacked my bum hard. This was definitely a side I hadn't seen before and I liked it! I felt him getting harder inside of me which reawakened my arousal.

I wished I could untie my hands and play with myself, but it certainly made the whole experience more tantalising. He moaned loudly and pulled out quickly. "Oh god," he said breathless. He flopped next to me, "I'll untie you as soon as I catch my breath," he panted. I twisted to my side and rested my hands above my head. "Maybe I'll just leave you like that all night," he teased. "You could, but then I would end up wetting the bed." "Ok, I'll untie you," he said. He gave me a gentle kiss on my forehead as he reached up to undo the knot.

I could no longer ignore my feelings for Jeremy. He was so attentive and sweet, we had the same interests and those curls were just so damn sexy. In contrast to the rough act of intimacy, he wrapped me in his arms and squeezed me tight. "I think I'm falling in love with you," he whispered in my ear. I squeezed him back and said, "I was just thinking about how much I'm falling for you." "I wish you didn't have to go back to Mallorca when we arrive," he said. "Well, maybe I don't," I replied.

CHAPTER 48

The next day, we finished the necessary pre-departure preparations and set sail to make our way across the Atlantic. The forecast called for easterly winds making great conditions for a downwind sail. We set up the spinnaker in port and hoped for an accurate forecast. The brightly shining sun added to the cheery ambiance. This would be the longest leg of our journey with no more stops, no pausing, just pure ocean.

All of us were on the flybridge in good spirits, laughing and joking and dancing to the upbeat music playing. Around 12 hours into the sail, a couple of whales joined us and played in the four meter waves behind us. The wind kept its promise and we flew the spinnaker. The royal blue sail sucked in the air and her fullness made for a tranquil sight in front of us.

During the long passage, Jeremy wanted to keep the three sides of blinds open so that he could monitor the weather and keep an eye on the spinnaker whilst lying in bed. This suited me fine as I love waking up to the sunlight. However, it meant there would be no orgasmic activities during the day since people would be walking around the bow and could see us. Night time was a different story. With the lights off, I could ride Jeremy while watching the stars guiding us west. I looked forward to the full moon so I could bathe in the mystical moon light while lying in the luxurious bed like a Queen.

Jeremy's watch was after mine so I often stayed up an extra hour to spend time with him and watch the evening sky. Sometimes I caught 40 winks in his lap while he ran his fingers through my hair and sang quietly along to his music. As there were now two couples onboard, the crew made an agreement that the flybridge was off limits in the evening. The romance of the open sea and starry night sometimes makes it impossible not to enhance the experience by orgasmic proportions.

As we sailed towards the middle of the ocean, the weather became warmer and my imagination started to run wild. There is something about an endless sea and starry night that I find so arousing. Who am I kidding? I'm nearly always aroused! One evening I reminded him of the "no knock, no entry" system we had in place.

As he was a newer captain, he was constantly worried the others would think he's unprofessional by being sexually involved with me. I drew my hands to his belt. "Brizo, come on. What if Seamus comes up for some fresh air?" "Don't worry, he won't come up here," I coaxed. It wasn't easy to break his resolve and after some protest, he allowed me to unbutton his trousers. I gently searched for his cock and stroked his growing excitement. It was an awkward grip as he didn't want to pull his trousers down any further. I teased the tip of his cock with the tip of my tongue and slowly, gently and sensually circled the top, going further and further down the length of his shaft.

When I sensed his body relax, I took his whole cock in my mouth. With my lips covering my teeth, I moved up and down his shaft barely touching him. I felt his body relax even more into the rhythm of my gentle movements. I gradually put more and more pressure on his cock while sucking gently. He put his hand on my head and whispered, "Oh that feels so good." I took this as encouragement and sucked harder, moving my hand faster and faster. I felt his body tense as it does just

~ 214 ~

before he orgasms. "Oh god," he whispered in excitement and I felt my mouth filling up with his salty liquid.

I swallowed and smiled at him. "There, now that wasn't so bad, was it?" I asked. "Yeah, whatever, we were just lucky," he said. He pulled me close to him. "Nope, I'm going to bed. Captain's privilege to receive a blow job from the stew," I winked at him. "Don't you want some pleasure?" he politely asked. "No way! I'm not going to get caught with my pants down!" I teased as I walked down the stairs. I did my usual run and jump onto the bed, feeling pretty proud that I gave Captain Jeremy his first blow job at the helm.

We had a mix of weather along the way. I had the privilege of seeing my first full rainbow. We actually went underneath a rainbow and at one point, one end of the rainbow started coming closer and closer so that the end was next to us. It was so close it felt like we could touch it. I screamed and jumped on deck, it was the most magical thing I had ever seen!

Jeremy was on the flybridge and shouted down to me. "Hey, there's a pot of gold at the end of the rainbow." I looked at him confused. "From this angle, you're at the end of the rainbow." I threw my head back in laughter. Sometimes Jeremy was super cheesy with his one-liners, but there was something so sincere no matter how bad the joke was.

Seamus loved to talk about sex. He enjoyed giving me suggestions as to what I should teach the young Jeremy. I loved the way he made me laugh and more than once thought how disappointing it was that he had a girlfriend. He definitely would have been my number one choice. After all, he was more age appropriate then Jeremy and not only am I a sucker for someone who makes me laugh, but if they can cook as well, I'm like putty in their hands. In one of our private conversations, he confided that sometimes he goes to the side of the boat at night to get some fresh air in solitude. I stopped what I was doing and my eyes became wide, "Really?" "Oh yeah, I see what you guys get up to," he winked.

There was a chance he could see us because whilst most of the time we had the lights off for that reason, if it was two or three in the morning, we sometimes left the lights on. "Really?" I repeated. "Nah, I'm just fucking with ya," he said as he carried on with that day's delicious treat. "Or am I?" he said with a raised eyebrow. I placed my hands over my mouth and eyes and muffled, "Oh my god, really?" "Maybe..." he teased.

I was mortified! Or was I? After all, he was good looking, hilarious and an amazing cook. I became turned on by the thought of him watching us. Based on our conversation, I made sure the lights were on that evening. My orgasm was extra intense as I rode Jeremy to thoughts of Seamus outside having a private little show. I made sure to arch my back further than usual. Just in case...

CHAPTER 49

After a sex filled journey across the ocean in that massive bed, we reached our final destination. In the last couple of days, Jeremy and I discussed our future. Due to the age gap, we knew that it wasn't going to last forever, but at the same time, we weren't ready for it to end yet. We came to the agreement that I would tie up some loose ends in Mallorca before flying back to Antigua where the boat would be docked in between charters and we could carry on our love affair.

ADONIS

CHAPTER 50

When I arrived back in Mallorca, Tyson, still trying to win me back, messaged to say that an acquaintance he knows needed someone to clean the boat he runs once or twice a week. I had met this captain, Adonis, at a BBQ earlier in the year and instantly felt a connection to him. Although I was with Tyson at the time and Adonis married, I remember thinking to myself, "Why are all the good men taken? He's so sweet and thoughtful and his dog is so fucking adorable!"

He had incredibly gorgeous eyes and a plethora of spare warm items for me to use when I came ill prepared for an outdoor BBQ on a cold spring's evening. I called Adonis and we agreed a day for me to come to the boat. "I'm only here for a few weeks," I informed him on the phone. "Yeah, that's cool. It would be nice to have a break from doing everything myself," he replied.

I was surprisingly nervous turning up at the boat. Not only because I hoped he would hire me again, but also because I remembered the jolt that went through my body when our hands accidentally touched at the BBQ. After showing me where all the deck cleaning supplies were, he said, "I just have to do some boring paperwork and then I'll come out and help you." "Ok, no problem," I said. The boat was tiny compared to the ones I had been working on, so I didn't think it would take that long anyway.

An hour later, Adonis came out and asked how I was. He picked up a sponge, "How far have you gotten?" After showing him how much I'd done, we carried on scrubbing away in silence.

"How's your wife?" I asked. The silence was awkward and that was the first icebreaker that came to me. "Actually, we've separated." "Oh I'm really sorry to hear that," I said sympathetically. "Don't be, it was my choice," he said. I turned away from him to hide my smile and eyebrow raise with the prospect that he was single.

"Lunch is part of the day rate, let's go somewhere to eat. I'm starving," Adonis said at 12.30. "Ok," I said. We took the dog and walked to the nearest restaurant/cafe. Adonis ordered a salad whilst I ordered something in Mallorquin I didn't understand. As we waited for our food to arrive, Adonis chatted non stop about his family and how he ended up in Mallorca. He didn't really ask me any questions, but I didn't mind because I was afraid I would have to reveal the Jeremy boyfriend issue. It was silly really, because I was probably going to work with him maybe one more time before I went back to the Caribbean.

We finished the work day a bit early because he had to meet a friend of his at his garage. Adonis was on a bike and I had to use the marina toilets, so we went our separate ways on the dock. As I started to walk away Adonis called out, "Hey Brizo!" "Yeah?" "I have two extra bikes in my garage if you want to borrow one while you're here for the next couple of weeks." "Thanks, that would be great! I'm out of town the next few days but I'll call you when I'm back," I replied. I turned around, rushing to the bathroom and thought to myself, "Hmmm clever way to make sure he sees me again." Still, I had committed to Jeremy for the time being and I wasn't one to cheat.

When I returned to Palma, I met Adonis at his garage and picked up a bike. As I arrived, a friend of his was just leaving. He briefly introduced us, his friend left and then he gave me a tour of his man cave. It was clearly his prized possession.

He nervously chatted away, "I'm going to convert this into a flat. The bed is going to go here, I'm going to make a shower room here and if you come outside in the back, I'm going to put some astroturf here and a deep mini pool over here. What do you think?" "Sounds cool," I lied. Even converted, it was still very much a garage with hardly any natural lighting and there were tower blocks hovering over the back garden. He seemed so excited about it, I couldn't burst his bubble. He showed me his motor bikes and stood next to me to show me a photo of a view during the ride he had that day. As I was looking at the photo, a message from the friend who just left popped up, "So you taking her for dinner?" he quickly swiped it away, but I had already seen it. I pretended as if I didn't and kept my smile internal.

Not long after I cycled home, a text from Adonis popped up, "Did the bike work ok? Are you home safe?" "Yeah, I had to walk it up the last part of the big hill because I'm unfit, but I'm home now," I replied. "Cool. There's a BBQ at the goat house tomorrow, do you want to come? I think we're hiking beforehand." "Yeah, that would be really nice," I said. Most of the friends I had in Mallorca where either in the Caribbean or had moved off the island, so I didn't have much to do.

The next morning, Adonis picked me up in his car. His sweet dog was also in the back. "What's your dog's name again?" "Sirius." "Oh yeah, that's right. He's so cute." We picked up a friend of his and drove into the enchanting mountains of Mallorca. Sirius led the three of us up the mountain to an old abandoned castle. The views were amazing. Endless terraced olive groves covered the valley with the Mediterranean Sea in the background. Rays of sun glistened off the water. Sirius sat close to me and I couldn't help but scooch closer so I could cuddle him. Maybe one day I would be cuddling Adonis too I thought mischievously. "I don't even like hiking. If you guys weren't here, I wouldn't come. What's the point of walking when there are cars and motorbikes?" Adonis said. I laughed and rolled my eyes. That was one tick against him.

Adonis was incredibly attentive and I could tell he fancied me. A nervous smile emerged when he talked to me and he was always concerned about my well being and comfort. He had eight years on me and was a gentleman without being chauvinistic. From the moment I met him at that BBQ, I felt protected and looked after in his presence.

"Did I make the right decision buying a ticket back to Antigua?" I thought quietly to myself. He had an air of confidence that was incredibly appealing. From the tour he gave me of his garage, it was obvious he was good at making things with his hands and I was desperate to know if that skill carried over into the bedroom. Don't get me wrong, I could teach and sculpt Jeremy to do what I wanted, but it's even more attractive when a man does it without instruction.

We joined four of their friends at the goat house. I thought the goat house was a restaurant, but it turned out to be one of his friend's land in the countryside. There was a small shepherd's hut on the side of a hill surrounded by olive trees. The view was gorgeous and we were far from any traffic and noise of other humans. The crowd was young, which didn't bother me, considering my boyfriend was 15 years younger than me.

"Sirius, stop that! Enough!" Adonis shouted. I looked over and saw Sirius trying to hump an empty shopping bag. "Now, now. Just because you're not getting any action doesn't mean that Sirius can't get any either," I teased. "Well that answers the question all of us were wondering," one of his friends remarked. "You guys aren't sleeping together then." We all laughed and Adonis looked over at me muttering, "Thanks for that." I giggled harder. We carried on into the evening drinking, smoking and passing joints. It was a really lovely day. Adonis was growing on me and my doubts about going to the Caribbean to play with my boy toy were getting stronger.

JEREMY PART 2

CHAPTER 51

Jeremy was flat out on a Christmas and New Year charter, so we didn't chat much when I was in Mallorca. During one of our brief conversations, I mentioned that Adonis and I had been out for dinner that evening and I was tipsy from all the wine. "You seem to be hanging out with Adonis quite a lot," he commented. "Yeah, he's nice. I don't have many friends here and his dog is super sweet," I replied. "Nothing is going on, he's exactly twice your age. I know who I'd rather choose," I said not being entirely honest.

I had been fighting an internal battle about what I should do. Jeremy was sweet, attentive and absolutely hilarious. I loved spending time with him and he naturally put a smile on my face. Adonis wasn't as funny, but he was sweet and attentive too. Since I already had the flight to Antigua booked, I decided to stick with my original plan. "People change their minds all the time," I fooled myself.

Adonis offered to drive me to the airport, but it didn't sit right with me. I made my own way and fell asleep on the plane excited that when I stepped off, I would be welcomed with intense sunshine and equally as intense chilled vibes. I was going to be on my own for one week before Jeremy sailed back into port. I rented a cute little shack outside of the harbour, far away from the parties and loud music. I instantly fell in love with the place and drifted off to dreamland to the soothing croaking of the tree frogs. I received the occasional text from Adonis, usually with the caveat he knew I would come around to him one day.

After what seemed like weeks, the day came when Jeremy was sailing into port. I was dripping with excitement, but also nervous to see him again. I put on my favourite onesie I bought at a boutique in Ibiza. It was a white and blue lacey number with little tassels hanging down from the short shorts. Wearing it made me feel chic, sexy and sophisticated. I sauntered to the marina at snail's pace so as not to induce any sweat. I hadn't had any action in a month, so that was the first thing on my agenda.

The boat came into view and my juices started flowing as I watched him slide in perfectly next to the dock. Seeing a guy handle big boats smoothly always gets me going. If he can drive a boat well, what else does he operate with confidence? Jeremy seemed a bit stand offish with his first hello, but they had just come off a long charter and then went straight into an 18 hour sail.

After they tied up, Jeremy took his time jumping down to give me a hug. It wasn't until Seamus said, "Go on! Off you go to kiss your girl," that he hopped off. He gave me a hug and awkward kiss. "Hmmm...what was going on here?" I thought. Jeremy told me to wait on the boat while he went to the office to sort the entry paperwork.

After what felt like forever, Jeremy came back onboard and I followed him to his cabin. "Oh, I'm so tired. I didn't get any rest because I had to deal with the fucking engine." I climbed on top of him, "Don't worry, you just have to lie there and I'll do the work Captain." I unbuckled his belt and worked my way towards the end of the bed. I grabbed his trousers and he lifted his hips for me to slide them off with ease. He pulled off his boxer shorts and slid them the rest of the way off as I kissed my way up his legs.

I was so excited to have him in my hands again. I kissed him all the way up to his lips, stopping for a teasing lick of his cock. He quietly moaned and grabbed my hair to pull me up to his face quicker. Our mouths opened and our tongues once again intertwined. He had such soft delicate kisses, they always got me so wet. I had all these visions of a long slow passionate reunion, but now that I was with him and feeling his muscular chest and biceps, I just wanted to fuck him immediately. "Can you unzip me please?" His hands found their way to my back to unzip the top part of my onesie. I sat up and finished unzipping the rest, throwing my beautiful costume on the floor. Now the only thing making me feel sexy was my own skin.

I climbed back on top of Jeremy and sat down on him. I was yearning to have him inside me, he couldn't get deep enough and I couldn't feel enough of him in me. I started circling my hips as if I was screwing him deeper into me. I was so wet, so excited and I couldn't restrain myself. I dropped my head back, closed my eyes and grinded hard and fast. I heard the familiar groan of his orgasm and put my finger on my clit as I was nearing orgasm and wanted to go on this journey with him.

It didn't take long, just a few circles with my middle finger and my release began. I quietly moaned as I climaxed, so as not to disturb the other crew members, even though they knew what we were doing. I climbed off Jeremy and laid next to him. "Well, that was a nice welcome," Jeremy said. "I'm sorry to do this to you, but I have to rinse down the boat and do some other things."

"I can stay and help you if you want," I volunteered.
"Awww...you don't have to. I can't pay you." "I know, but if I help, you're done faster and then we can have fun." I brought extra shorts with me in case he wanted help. I borrowed one of his work shirts and went on deck. It felt so nice to be back with him, but I wasn't getting the impression he was as excited to be back with me.

CHAPTER 52

A couple of weeks later, Jeremy picked me up from work to enjoy sunset at the beach. He spotted one of his friends enjoying a thirst quenching pina colada. He seemed unusually excited to see her, "Do you mind if we sit with you?" he asked. I thought this was strange as we hadn't been spending much time together recently. "Sure, but a friend of mine is coming in a minute, so more people will be coming." "The more the merrier," he replied.

They were chatting away about some mutual friends and I went to the shore to soak my legs in the refreshing sea. The next day was Valentine's Day and I wasn't feeling the love from Jeremy. I was lost in my own thoughts about what to do. I startled with the feel of a hand on my shoulder. "Hey," he said with that pantie dropping smile. "You alright?" I shrugged my shoulders, not really knowing what to say. He put his arm around me and tapped my lower back like you would do to a friend. "You're not really into me anymore, are you Jeremy?" "No, Brizo. I'm sorry, but I'm not." I nodded my head, "Ok, I thought so."

He explained himself as he drove me home. "I guess I just got lost in the excitement of it all in the beginning. It's hard for me to focus on my work when I'm worried about having to call and text you and I just haven't been doing my job properly." I later regretted asking the question, "Anything else?" "To be honest, I think I just need to be with someone my age. You looked older than I remembered. When I saw you on the dock, I couldn't help but notice your old lady knees." My head snapped round to look at him, "Alright, no need to be so honest. Some things are left better unsaid!" I said defensively.

Before Jeremy left the island for the winter, he called and asked if I wanted to meet up for one last drink. One drink turned into three and we were laughing and having a good time. Upon accepting the invitation, my intention was to get him drunk in hopes that he would spend the night with me.

Sure enough, in the middle of the third drink, he reached his hand across the table and grabbed mine, "Awww..Brizo, I'm sorry it didn't work out. You are a really cool chick. If only we were at different life phases." I smiled back at him, "Thanks Jeremy. That's really sweet. Are you going to come back to mine or what?" I winked. "Of course. We both knew that was going to happen after the second drink. Should we go?" "Fuck, I just shelled out all that money for a third drink when you were already mine?" I said with a sparkle in my eye.

Back at the love shack, I closed the door and was immediately shoved into it. Jeremy put his hands on either side of my head and gave me a passionate breathtaking kiss. He pulled up my dress and hurriedly pulled my underwear down. As he bent down to take them off, his tongue caressed my clitoris. "Ooooo..." I moaned in surprise. I hadn't ever seen this spontaneous side of him before and I loved it!

After ensuring my pussy was ready to set sail, he grabbed my hand and pulled me towards the bed. He took my dress off and unsnapped my bra before pushing me back on the bed. He carried on licking my pussy using firm quick strokes that were sending me into ecstasy. I grabbed those luscious locks with both of my hands and pushed his head further into me.

Eventually he stopped and laid down on the bed. I started moving towards his cock to repay the oral pleasure. "Just fuck me," he commanded. "Whatever you say captain," I said, as I gently lowered my warm moist pleasure box onto his stiff mast. The unexpected passion and tongue play with my clit had gotten me more than ready. Luckily, he was just as ready and after a few deep long thrusts, we reached orgasm at the same time. I flopped down onto his chest, "I'm really going to miss that," I said breathlessly.

The next morning, he woke early and kissed my naked back. "Have a good rest of your winter," he said. Although I knew all along this was never going to last forever, I was still heartbroken it was ending so soon. "At least we went out with a bang," I announced to thin air

SIMON

CHAPTER 53

"Ok, see you tomorrow!" Finally! After a week of walking around the marinas asking boats if they were hiring, I received a reply. I would be helping a boat prepare for racing. I had never worked on a race boat before and it was something I had always wanted to do. Have you ever seen the crew on those boats? They are full of fit, muscular men. It couldn't have come at a better time. Jeremy had just left and I was determined not to waste any time finding a new sailor for this port.

When I rocked up on my first day, the deck was teeming with big strong sailors. My heart started racing with nerves. I dropped my shoulders back and puffed my chest out trying to hide my nervousness with confidence. "I'm here to see Catherine," I asked the first guy who acknowledged my presence. It was intimidating being the new girl with 15 gorgeous muscular guys walking around deck. Catherine came out and invited me aboard. She explained what we had to do in the next week and let me get on with it. Once the guys realised I would be working all week, they asked my name and made little jokes whenever they passed by.

My second day onboard, I was packing away the galley equipment when a wave of loneliness passed over me and tears welled up in my eyes. I knew if I didn't say anything I would burst into tears, so I asked Marie, the chef, "What are you up to this weekend?" "Oh, I'm renting a car and going off by myself. I spend all week here and I just like to be on my own and get away from the crew." "That sounds cool. I've never left the harbour!" "Really? You should. It's a beautiful island. What are you doing this weekend?" she asked.

The tears were welling up uncontrollably now. "I don't know. My boyfriend and I just broke up a couple of days ago and all my friends are on charter." "Oh honey!!" she said as she came over to give me a hug. "Don't worry, there are plenty of other fish in the sea. This island is the best place to be single," she assured me.

"Hey, can anyone with small hands help me?" Simon said as he flew down the companionway. Marie had her hands full prepping race crew food, "Are my hands small enough?" I asked. "Let me see?" I held up my hands. "Sure, let's give it a try." I followed him on deck. "How are you with climbing the mast?" he asked. "No problems whatsoever," I replied. "Cool." He showed me the best foot positioning to climb on to the boom. He scurried off to the end and I quickly followed. "So I dropped this part in here and I can't get my hand in deep enough. Does your hand fit? Can you grab it?" I stuck my hand down and after some difficulty, accomplished the task. He grabbed my hands and yelled, "Yeesssss!!! Thank you so much! You're a life saver. I owe you some beers." I turned around and at that point, realised just how thin the boom was, but tried to play it cool and walk off as quickly as I had walked on. I strived to be the cool sailor, as I sensed many pairs of eyes watching me.

The next day, Marie and I were alone in the galley. "So I talked to Simon last night and if you're lonely, I think he would be keen to meet up," Marie said. "Oh really? I don't know. I'll think about it." "Well at least take his number." She picked up her phone and read out his number. Later that night when I got home, I thought about whether or not I was ready to meet up with someone else so soon. "Fuck it!" I picked up the phone and texted Simon, "So when are you going to take me out for those beers you promised?" "Hey, I'm on watch tonight, but we're all going out tomorrow. Come with!" he replied a few hours later. A Friday night out with his crew suited me just fine!

CHAPTER 54

I spent forever getting ready, changing my outfit three times. I even put on fancy underwear for the occasion. I wasn't planning on revealing all, but just in case, you never know! I walked up the stairs and the music got louder and louder as I walked towards the entrance of the busy bar. The dance floor was lit up with colourful disco lights spinning around the floor, walls and ceilings.

I didn't see Simon, but I spotted some crew from another boat I had worked on. My friend Julia spotted me from across the room and we put our most serious faces on as we shook our hips and chest to meet in the middle of the dance floor. We screamed out a huge hello and gave each other a big hug. "What do you want to drink? It's on me!!" Julia shouted over the blaring music. "Gin and sparkling water with lime please!" I shouted back. We sipped our drinks and caught up about boys in between dancing to the good songs. Julia was full of fun stories about this summers conquests.

Suddenly I felt a tap on my shoulder and turned around to see Simon. "Hey!" he said embracing me. "You alright?" "Yeah, I'm good thanks," I shouted back. He pointed to his glass and I shook my head yes. "What are you drinking?" he asked with his hand around my waist. I couldn't help but burst into a big smile, "Gin and sparkling water with lime." "Ok, that's weird. Are you sure you don't want tonic?" he asked, squeezing my waist. His touch sent tingles up my spine. "I'm good," I laughed.

Julia and I carried on chatting while Simon got the drinks. He handed me my drink and went over to chat to his friends. "Glad

You Came," by the Wanted came blasting out of the speakers. Julia and I jumped to the rhythm of the music and laughed away as we displayed our most ridiculous dance moves.

Simon came up behind me and put his arms around me, slowing me down to a gentle sway. "Do you want to go outside for a cigarette?" he asked. It was a great excuse to get outside so that I could actually have a conversation without having to yell. I nodded my head and followed him outside.

Simon pointed at the hotel across the way, "I've booked a hotel room for the weekend. I'm so fucking sick of staying on the boat. Sharing a cabin and hitting the wall every time I move around. I'm fucking over it." "Nice. What are the rooms like?" I asked. "Ahhh...mate, it's so nice! I have a little kitchenette so I can make spaghetti Bolognese and a full English breakfast. I have a balcony with a view over the harbour. It's fucking mint. Fucking expensive, but totally worth it!" "Nice." "Maybe you can come check it out," he said as he lifted his eyebrow. I smiled and coquettishly shrugged my shoulders. "If you're lucky," I winked.

We went back inside and carried on dancing. The drinks were flowing and it didn't take me long to start seeing double. I flitted between groups of friends, laughing and joking with Julia and dancing and flirting with Simon.

Suddenly the music softened and the bartender shouted in an Antiguan accent, "Go home! Grab the nearest guy or girl and enjoy the rest of your evening!" Simon reappeared and asked if I wanted to do some cocaine. "Sure? Why not!" Of course it was a great idea when I was pissed. "Come with me."

I followed Simon outside and we walked towards the car park. "Just wait here," he said. My friends were close behind us. "Hey Brizo! What's going on?" Julia said. "Just waiting for Simon," I said raising my eyes. "Really? Let me know how it goes," she said bumping my shoulder with hers. "Fuck!! I'm so drunk and I just really want my bed. Why does it take so long for everyone to leave?!?" slurred Julia.

Simon came running into view and put his arm around me. Julia walked back towards her crew. "So we have to wait like an hour," said Simon. "Ok," I replied. "Let's go sit by the water because he can't come into the hotel." I followed him to the dinghy dock. We flicked off our flip flops and dangled our feet in the water. He sat close to me and leaned in to kiss me. He was an aggressive kisser, but I kind of liked it. It was clear that he was in charge. He grabbed my hair with his hand and pulled it down so the rest of my body followed. We were both lying on the uncomfortable dock, him on his side and me on my back but I was too busy enjoying being submissive to notice the discomfort. His free hand alternated between my chest and my groin with confident strokes. I gasped a moan, wow it felt so good to be devoured by such strong hands.

Subtle vibrations on the dock interrupted our lustful act. "Simon?" a voice shouted. We quickly sat up and looked over, "Ah, hey!" Simon acknowledged. "Just a sec Brizo." As I went to move my leg, I knocked one of his flip flops in the sea. "Oh shit!" I exclaimed trying to grab it with my foot. The disturbance in the water made it float off in the opposite direction to us. "Fuuuccckkk!" "Jump in!" I giggled. "No fucking way," Simon replied. "Sorry!" I said placing my hand over my mouth. I thought about jumping in, but I would've had to walk home for spare clothes which was 20 minutes in the opposite direction from his hotel. "Fuck, don't worry about it. I'll be right back," he said as he walked off wearing one flip flop.

A few minutes later Simon came back. "Alright, I got some candy. Should we do a line now or do you want to go back to the hotel?" he asked. "Let's do one now," I said. Memories of St Martin came flooding back. Specifically, Matthieu snorting lines off my ass before he fucked me from behind. Mmmm...I was getting wet just thinking about what would happen in the next half hour.

Simon cut a line for each of us on a card from his wallet and took the first one. He passed it over to me and said, "Ah cool, it's good shit. This guy never disappoints." I sniffed the erotic juice and waited for it to enter my bloodstream. "Not bad," I said. Although I was so drunk, I didn't really notice if it was good or bad. Within seconds, I felt the familiar heightened sense of confidence and urge to spread my wisdom non stop. My verbal diarrhoea exploded as we walked back to the hotel room. Simon proudly gave me the grand tour of his suite. I had visions of warm streams of water shooting over my head as I looked at the massive inviting shower. It was far superior to the chambers my freelancer budget could afford.

"I have a couple of beers, want one? We can drink it on the balcony and admire the view." "Oooo.. yeah, let's enjoy the view." I said. I walked out to the balcony and breathed in the sight of the rocking yachts. Simon came out with the beer and his speaker. He turned on some catchy techno tunes and we toasted. "Cheers. Thanks for the invite. It's a nice place to sleep compared to what I'm used to," I said with a smile. "Nah, thanks for coming. It would be a shame to have this big room all to myself. We can make spaghetti tomorrow if you want to stick around." He said this as he cut up more lines of coke on the table.

Simon rolled up a dollar bill and handed it to me. "Want another one?" I took the bill and inhaled more powder confidence. "You're so far away," I said as he took his turn and folded the bill back in his wallet. I stood up from my chair and straddled him. I wrapped my arms around his neck. "That's better," I smiled. I leaned in for a kiss and he again grabbed my hair and gently tugged it down. It must be his signature trick. Luckily, I really like getting my hair pulled.

Enrique Iglesias blared sexily from the speaker. "Ooooo! I love this song!" I screeched. The cocaine was surging through my system now, giving me the confidence of a porn star. I started giving him a lap dance. Unfortunately, I was wearing the sexy onesie that I wore for Jeremy's arrival, so I couldn't strip my top off and swing it around my head. I reached behind to unzip the onesie. "Need some help?" Simon said eagerly. "Yeah, I think so." He undid the top of the zip and I slid the rest of it down. I placed my finger under one strap and let it elegantly fall off my shoulder while moving my arm out to reveal what was underneath. I switched hands and did the same on the other side. "Nice moves," Simon said with a smile. "Thanks. I took six months of burlesque classes in London. Guess they're finally paying off," I giggled. I unhooked my bra and threw it to the side.

I reached in for a kiss and was startled by a noise as the door to the side of the balcony started opening. We both looked over in shock. I quickly placed my hands on my breasts. A woman appeared, "Can you please turn the music down. It's three in the morning and we have children sleeping over here." "Oh, sure sorry about that!" said Simon, quickly reaching to turn off his speaker. "Thanks so much," she said closing the door. We both looked at each other and giggled quietly. "Holy fuck! I can't believe that!" Simon whispered. "She saw my fucking tits! That was only supposed to be for you!" I whispered through hysterics. "Should we go inside now?" Simon asked. "Good idea," I said climbing off of him.

We snickered our way back into the room. I let my onesie fall down to my ankles and stepped out of it. Simon took off his shorts and pushed me over on the bed. He stuck two fingers inside of me and vigorously moved them in and out. The alcohol had dehydrated my pussy and despite gagging to have him inside of me, my body reactions weren't cooperating with my sexual urges. He stuck his fingers deeper inside of me and rubbed my clit with his thumb. Finally! My natural lubrication made an appearance and Simon jumped at the opportunity. He clumsily pulled down his boxer shorts with his free hand. I looked down to see what was about to enter me. "Oh fuck!" I screamed. He paused a moment, "What?" "You're too fucking huge and I'm scared." He laughed and winked, "You like it, huh?" "No, I really don't. Not all girls like huge penises!" "Oh whatever," he said proudly and carried on revving my engine.

I started to push him off of me, "What are you doing?" he asked. "I want to suck your cock." "Hmmm...I want to fuck you," he replied. I was trying to prolong the inevitable, so instead of arguing with him, I laid back and forced myself to relax about the monstrosity that was about to enter me.

After enjoying his slightly aggressive foreplay, I was finally wet enough to accept a visitor. He went on his knees and lifted my hips so that he could get a deep angle. He bulldozed his way in deep. "Ahhh...that feels so good," he moaned softly, pausing at the deepest point. "Just go slow," I moaned. He threw my legs up on either side of his ears and held on to my legs for leverage. He thrusted slow and deep. I grabbed his knees to keep him deeper in me. The cocaine porn star side of me was coming out and I was screaming loudly, "Fuck me harder, faster," I demanded. "Oh that's so good, you can't get deep enough," I encouraged. The commentary was forcing him to thrust harder and deeper.

Suddenly he pulled out of me, flinging my legs to the side. He flopped down on the bed and grabbed me. "Get on top and fuck me girl," he ordered. I eagerly did so. I was frothing with arousal and confidence. I grinded him hard, rotating my hips round and round. I arched my back and placed my hands on his thighs, thrusting my pelvis further forward to get a different angle. "Oh god, this is good," he shouted between my moans and groans.

I really did feel like a porn star. I wished someone was filming our animalistic carnage. I felt like a sex goddess and wanted everyone to see how much I was enjoying this. Simon put his thumb on my clit. The extra stimulation was tingling through me and I started to peak. "Oh god, oh god, oh god. Simon I'm so fucking close. Ooooohhhh, it feels like fucking heaven," I shouted. I sat straight back up on his cock, placing my hands on his chest to hold on while I climaxed. I knew it was going to be intense. "I'm about to come," I moaned. "Go for it," he egged on. "No, I don't want to, this feels too fucking good," I protested. "Go on, I'll just fuck you again." Those words sent me into my own little world.

I closed my eyes and focused on thrusting my hips further forward. A tingling sensation rushed to my groin and an electric sensation ran through my whole body. The cocaine intensified the feeling and I knew I was going to come hard. I grabbed his chest, dropped my head back and screamed, "I'm coming, I'm coming, oh my god I'm coming so hard!!" I felt his hips beneath mine, either excited from the pure ecstasy I was experiencing or in order to try and come with me.

After what felt like longer than usual, I exclaimed, "Wow. I'm still coming." I felt every centimetre of my pussy throbbing as I reached my final release. His thrusts became slower. "Hold on. That was so intense. I just need a minute," He wore a proud smile, "No worries. My pleasure," he replied. "No, it was really mine," I said closing my eyes and dropping my head back. His hands came up to my nipples and started squeezing them. "Not to worry, when you're ready, I'll keep going and do it again."

Simon pushed my hips up and threw me to the side of the massive king sized bed. He twisted me over to my stomach grabbed my hips and pulled them back towards him. "I hope you're ready because I can't wait any longer." "Go ahead," I whispered. He came in from behind, only sticking in the tip of his hard cock, "Is that ok?" he asked. "Fuck me as you wish." "Oh my god," he whispered and started thrusting in and out fast, pulling my hips back and forth. Just as I started playing with my clit to enjoy another orgasm, he pulled out and I felt his warm liquid oozing down my back. "Sorry. Your pussy just felt too fucking good and I couldn't hold it anymore." Out of breath, we flopped onto our backs.

Simon reached over to turn off the light. "Oh look, it's getting light outside," I said, noticing the dawn glow pour in from the side of the curtains. "I'm going to watch the sunrise." I found one of his t-shirts to throw on. I stepped into my underwear and walked outside, leaving the French doors wide open. The sun crept up behind the hotel, shedding a golden light on the green and luscious hills in front of us. Simon pranced out in his boxer shorts and lit a cigarette. "It's fucking beautiful," he said. "It sure is. It's my favourite part of boating life," I said. "All of the beautiful sunrises and sunsets we get to see in different parts of the world." "Yeah, that's definitely a perk," he agreed.

We sat outside chatting about random shit for I don't know how long. "The rugby is playing in a few hours, so I should try and get some sleep. Want to snuggle next to me in the air con?" he asked. "Sure." I'm not sure how long it took to get to sleep, but I woke up to the sound of his alarm. "Fuck, I'm so tired," Simon whined. "Just stay here then," I said snuggling closer to him. "No way, it's going to be a good game. I'll drink a couple of beers and feel better," he said. I dozed on and off while Simon took a shower and got dressed. He leaned over the bed and gave me a kiss. "I'm going now, but feel free to stay here as long as you want. Take a shower and do whatever you want. We can watch a movie after the game and I can make spag bol if you want to stay," Simon said. "Sure," I said smiling.

I heard the latch of the door click and suddenly I wasn't sleepy anymore. I stepped into the luxurious shower and let the water run down my head and satisfied body. I willed it to wash away the hangover as well as the shame I felt for using cocaine again. I opened my eyes and smiled at the opportunity to have such a superb shower and sleep in air conditioning. I stepped out of the shower and realised that I only had my goddess onesie with me and it wasn't comfortable enough to wear all day. I decided to go home and try to sleep a bit. I had plans to go out again that evening with Julia and her crew. Plus, Simon served his purpose. Besides cocaine and sex, we didn't really have a lot in common. I dressed and started the hot and sweaty 25 minute stride of pride to my house. Halfway home, I saw Aaron and his mate heading towards me on their skateboards. I cringed, "Hey guys!" I said as they got closer. "Hey," said Aaron. "I thought it was you." He gave me a confused look, "Just finished partying or what?" he said with a knowing chuckle. "Ummm...maybe," I giggled. "Are you still coming out tonight?" he asked. "I think so. I just have to take a nap first!" "Cool, we'll see you later. Get ready for tonight crazy girl!" Aaron said as they skated off.

ADONIS PART 2

CHAPTER 55

Alas came the time to cross the Atlantic and search for work on the European side. I found a delivery job on the biggest boat I had ever sailed on. The crew were all friendly and welcoming, however only myself and one of the other delivery crew were genuinely looking forward to the sail. The permanent crew were worn out from a chaotic season and were wishing for time off the boat instead of time trapped on the boat. I ignored their negativity and soaked in the solitude and serenity of the sea.

The whole time I was in Antigua, Adonis kept in contact. Often times I had totally forgotten about him and then out of the blue a text popped up reminding me that he was waiting for me on the other side of the ocean. After my Caribbean romps and flirts, I was looking forward to a bit of sea time to re-connect with myself.

"I found a boat crossing to Italy," I informed Adonis. "Oh great, you'll be in Europe." "Yeah, maybe our boats will be in the same port at the same time and we can meet up again," I texted back. "Does the boat have satellite internet?" Adonis asked. I rolled my eyes, I don't sail to be on my phone, I sail to connect with the ocean. "I don't know, but even if it does, I keep my phone off on deliveries," I replied. "What if I need to get a hold of you?" he asked. "You'll have to wait until I'm back on land," I replied.

The crossing was uneventful as far as weather and sailing goes, but full of drama with the captain and his wife. I just wanted to get off the boat. We were going to stop in Mallorca to check in to Europe. I told the captain I wasn't keen to stay and could either carry on the two days to Italy or he could leave me here and save the flight expense. The feeling was mutual as his response was to wave and shout an angry, "Bye!"

When we got closer to land, I turned my phone on and texted Adonis to see if he would be able to meet me at the dock. Despite it being a Friday, we were arriving early in the morning and I hoped his captain would be understanding and let him arrive to work a bit late. "Hold on, I'll send him a message so when he wakes up, he'll get it," he said. Adonis had his phone on 24-7, as if he was afraid to miss out on some important message.

"So what dock are you going to and what's your ETA?" he wrote. Yes!!!!! I felt my loins tingling with anticipation. He had been married for 13 years, surely he knew how to handle a woman in bed. I couldn't wait to feel those firm engineer hands fine tuning my body. "I hope you're a good kisser or it's over before it begins," I teased. It was a long two hours to port. We could see the mountains from miles away and the minutes passed by like hours. I felt like I was a race horse having a carrot dangled in front of me and I willed the finish line to come quicker. Not too quickly though...

We approached the dock at dawn. The sun still hadn't poked its head up. The sky was full of deep blues, dark reds and fiery oranges. As we got closer, I saw the silhouettes of Adonis and his dog, Sirius. My heart started racing and blood rushed to my cheeks. I was so excited to see him, but incredibly nervous. I had gained some weight in the last five months, maybe he wouldn't be as attracted to me.

Or what if the kiss was awful? Would I even want to try for more? I hadn't told any of my friends when I was arriving because Adonis said I could stay with him. Wait, what? I agreed to stay with a guy I had never even kissed? "Bow line first!" the captain shouted, pulling me back into the present moment. Adonis walked towards the bow to catch the line. The butterflies in my stomach started flying around like crazy. He walked towards me and caught my line as I flung it. "Hey sailor girl," he called out in his sexy South African voice. "Hi!" I smiled back.

As soon as the boat was secured, I jumped off and ran up for a huge hug. He gave me a peck on the lips, "Is that all?" I teased. "I'm not about public displays of affection," he said nodding his head at the crew behind us. I told some of the crew about us and they wanted to watch the sweet love story unfold before their eyes. I sat on the dock for a bit and when all eyes went inside, I reached over and gave him a kiss. "Yes, that's acceptable," I smiled. "I'm happy to find out what more you have to offer," I winked. He smirked and went in for another lock of the lips.

CHAPTER 56

Adonis brought me to his place and then had to go back to work. After 26 straight days at sea, I was exhausted. I fell asleep the minute my head hit the soft pillow. I woke up to the loud garage door being whipped open. I stretched my arms up over my head and gave Adonis a sleepy smile. He bent over to give me a kiss. I felt a warm sensation travel from my lips down to my groin. I pulled him closer to me wanting to feel more of him. He resisted, "I'm starving. Can I take a washed up sailor girl out for a nice dinner?" "Hmmm...Can we start with desert first?" I asked. "It will be better the longer we wait," he replied. "Come on. Get ready." I rolled my eyes and got up from the bed.

We went to one of the restaurants that we frequented together before I left for Antigua. It serves local tapas and overlooks the sea, with candles on all of the tables adding a tinge of romance to the air. Our chat was full of sexual innuendos. I could tell already that my sexual libido was going to be much higher than his. I couldn't keep my hands off of him and he seemed a bit unsure how to handle it.

At last, our wine saturated bodies could no longer contain the sexual tension. We staggered the long journey home, laughing and making several tongue twisting stops. His arm was wrapped around my waist and it felt so good and natural. I quickly fell in rhythm with his step. His arm was long and strong, making me feel protected. It was the most innocent foreplay I'd had since high school.

We arrived back at his place, where he took out candles and spread them around the room. "Ooooo, Mr Romantic!" I exclaimed. He raised one eyebrow than walked over to me and wrapped his protective arms around me. He lifted me up and brought me over to the bed where he gently laid me down. He kissed my neck before fumbling around to get my shirt off. It felt so awkward, yet so familiar at the same time. He slid his tongue around my nipples and gave them a little bite before kissing me to my belly button and beyond. Adonis pulled my jeans away from my belly and kissed as far down as he could reach. He unbuttoned my jeans and I helped him free Lady V, ready to be used as a playground in whichever way he wanted.

Adonis slid his hands underneath my thighs as if they were porcelain he didn't want to break. The tip of his pointy tongue flicked my sopping wet pussy sending shivers through my torso. My nipples hardened with excitement as the shiver carried upwards, bringing my chest with it. It escaped my body as a moan. I was pleasantly surprised at his skills as he played my pleasure key like a finely tuned piano. "You taste fucking amazing," he said as he tickled his beard on my clit. "You feel fucking amazing," I groaned. I enjoyed the dual sensation between his tongue and his beard and melted into the mattress. His tongue slithered up the middle of my body, I reached my head back to receive it on my bare neck. I slipped my arms around him as his tongue found its way into my mouth.

I was so lost in the ecstasy, I hadn't even realised that he had managed to undress himself. I felt his bare chest on mine and his hard cock rubbing against my groin. "I want to feel you inside of me," I whispered as I nibbled on his ear. "I'm not going to last very long, it's been way too long," he said and then snickered. I laughed along with him, "That's ok. We both have fingers if you make it around the buoy before I do." "Just shut up and get in me," I said as I stared deep into his eyes. Neither of us used our hands, I pushed up my hips and his throbbing cock found its way in. I grabbed his bum and brought him deeper in me, holding him there. The emotional intimacy had been building for five months now and it was time for the physical intimacy. I moved my hips beneath him, noticing how perfectly he fit inside of me. He slowly pumped in and out when all I wanted was for him to go quicker to build up the heat and passion between our most intimate parts. "Oh fuck," he said as his thrusts became deeper and slower and eventually he pulled out. "I'm so sorry!" he said in horror. "It's just been so long, I didn't think it would be that quick!!" I laughed, "Don't worry. I think we will have plenty of time for longer sessions." His tongue once again ran down my torso and found my sweet spot. I was drunk with arousal and his tongue was very talented. It seemed like within seconds, I grabbed his hair and screamed, "Oh Adonis!!" as my body shuddered with satisfaction.

CHAPTER 57

A month after I arrived, Adonis had to go to Italy for work. He tried to get me a job on the boat, but it was when I was crossing the Atlantic and had my phone off. The captain needed an answer before I arrived. However, he managed to get me to Italy because the boat needed a part ASAP and it was quicker for me to but it in Mallorca and fly it out to them. Adonis and I stayed alone on the boat while the rest of the crew stayed ashore.

I sailed with them back to Mallorca, but we anchored a couple of nights in Sardinia so the crew could recover and get the boat out of race mode. Adonis knows how much I love naked outdoor showers, so one night when the crew went to bed early, he said, "Want to risk a shower on the stern? There's a beautiful full moon." "Of course!" I squealed with excitement. We took our shower supplies to the stern and braced ourselves for the cool wind.

It felt so good after sweating in the sun in all day. Adonis held the shower head over me while I quietly screamed with the shock of the cold. We giggled as he continued to torture me with it. "Ok, stop, stop, I need to soap myself," I begged. As I slathered soap all over my naked body, I could see how the moonlight was lighting up my skin, my nipples hard from the cold water. Adonis quietly screamed with the shock of the cold shower, trying not to wake the crew. We sat there giggling under the moonlight, stealing kisses in between rinses.

"Do you need help washing Adonis Jr?" I asked seductively. "No, we can't do that out here. What if someone comes out!!

It's one thing if they see us shower, it's another if they see us in a sexual act." "Ok, Mr Boring," I retorted. When we finished, he wrapped my towel around me and put his arms around me kissing my head. "You're so fun and beautiful," he whispered in my ear. "I know," I replied cheekily. We went into the cabin and had a quiet love making session.

Adonis and I carried on seeing each other for a while, but after the last four years of sexual escapades I had been having, his libido just wasn't matched with what I had grown accustomed to. When I decided to go to the Caribbean later that year, I used it as the perfect excuse to end it.

DAVID

CHAPTER 58

I was back in Antigua for my second Caribbean season of frolicking around the beautiful tropical island, whilst waiting for work to come my way. I spent the mornings hiking and swimming at the beach to allow the sun to kiss my near naked body. When the tourists started arriving after their all inclusive breakfasts, I gathered my belongings and headed back home to get ready for the dreaded dock walking. I put on short, yet professional shorts, a tight top showing my cleavage and headed out with my smile and CV in hopes that I would get some work. Vain, I know, but that's the way the yachting industry works.

Luckily, I got a call from a Captain, Tony, who had advertised a stewardess job. I met him at the yacht and ended up having quite a long interview. As he showed me around the boat, he stopped at the crew quarters and said, "This is my cabin. I usually share it with the chef, but he's been here for years, so I'm thinking of giving him his own cabin as a reward. If you get the job, you would probably be sharing with me." They were having a big crew turnover, so he was having a rethink about the cabin arrangements. I discreetly lifted my eyebrow and thought to myself, "He wouldn't be bad to share a cabin with. I wonder how long it would take until we start sharing a bed..."

Sadly, the owner didn't like my CV, but Tony felt bad, so he made it his mission to find me work. "There's a boat crossing to Europe in March, it's my friend David. I'll give him your CV and you guys can have a chat," he said. "That's great! I love crossings," I said.

Later that night, I went to a dock party. I didn't really want to go as I didn't know anyone, but I knew it would be good for networking, so I sucked it up and went. Who knows, maybe I would find some new sailors to keep me entertained.

I turned up at the dock, found the person who invited me and sat down for a chat and a drink. People from neighbouring boats were coming and going all evening. At one point a short English guy with dark brown hair and intense brown, almost black eyes, sat next to me. "Hey, I'm David. What's your name?" I could tell from his English accent that he was a typical lad and I had passed that phase in my life. "I'm Brizo," I said in the most disinterested voice I could conjure up. He started talking about his boat and their season plans, I suddenly thought, "Oh shit, it's David! The David that the captain was telling me about." "Are you David, Tony's friend, who is looking for delivery crew?" I asked. "Yep, that would be me, why?" I said, "I'm Brizo, he said he was going to give you my CV." "Well even better, why don't you stop by the boat tomorrow and pass it to me yourself." "Will do!" I replied. "So Brizo, do you have a boyfriend?" he asked. I internally rolled my eyes as I pondered how to reply. "We just broke up." "Well, I'm sorry to hear that. He must be a destroyed man." "Ha, ha. Thanks," I said trying not to vomit in my mouth.

CHAPTER 59

The next day, I went to David's boat to drop off my CV as promised. They had finished work for the day and the crew were sat in the cockpit. David came onto the dock to chat with me, "There's a group of us going dinghy sailing on the weekend if you want to join," he asked after the business part of our conversation ended. "Yes of course, that would be great!" I said all too excitedly. "Great. Can I contact you on this number here?" he asked pointing to my CV. "Yep, that's the one."

The weekend arrived and I got a message from David. "My crew pussied out. They're all too hungover. I'm still up for getting out of the harbour. Can I take you to lunch somewhere?" Ugh, I don't really want to hang out with him alone, I thought to myself. Fuck it. "Sure. Just let me know what time and where I should meet you," I replied.

A few hours later, David and I drove out of the harbour. Despite having spent the previous winter there, I worked too much to explore the rest of the island. The drive was gorgeous. We drove through tiny little towns consisting of main streets lined with little shacks and eventually popped out to a rainforest. The sides of the road became more thickly lined with luscious green tropical trees as the houses and little towns disappeared. It felt like we had driven into another country. David was incredibly hilarious and we spent the 45 minute car journey bantering back and forth. Hmmm...maybe... I pondered. He wasn't really my type, but hey, there have been plenty of "not my type" guys I've ended up with. After all, the best way into my pants is through laughter. The laughter was certainly plentiful, that's for sure.

After driving through the humid fresh rainforest, dipping in to valleys and over hills, we arrived at the coastline. Although it was built up with luxury homes and hotels, there were pockets of rugged coastline, beautiful empty beaches and waves crashing along rocky shores. It was stunning and very romantic. We pulled up to a gated resort and were stopped by the security guard, "Do you have a reservation?" she said in that carefree Caribbean accent that relaxes me. "No, we don't. Any chance we can get one last minute?" David asked flirtatiously. "Let me see what I can do for ya," she replied. She walked away and made a phone call. "It's your lucky day. Go on in, they're reserving a table for you two." "Amazing, thanks," he replied.

The entrance to the resort was like walking into a tropical garden. Pink, white and yellow exotic flowers and palm trees disguised the buildings of the grounds. We got lost and had to ask a staff member where the restaurant was. Eventually the path opened up onto a deck overlooking the beach and a beautiful bay with that unique Caribbean turquoise sea. Distressed white tables dotted the deck, set with colourful flowers. Opaque white curtains loosely floated in the breeze and gentle reggae music set the tone for not having a care in the world.

"What would you like to drink? A cocktail or should we start with wine?" David asked. I had vowed I wasn't going to drink, but my resolve lasted all of three seconds. "It's hot outside. Rosé is always refreshing on a hot summer's day. Do you like rosé?" "Absolutely!" he replied. Seeing as it was only 12.30, I had a feeling this was going to be the start of a long day. I internally made a promise to behave myself.

The setting was beautiful and idyllic. Our table was at the edge of the beach and we watched sailboats gliding past in the picturesque turquoise water as we ate our lunch and quenched our thirst with rosé. We moved our third bottle of rosé to the sun loungers on the beach and went for a dip to cool down. The alcohol had induced heavy flirting between us, but I was still undecided if I wanted David to be my sailor in this port. After all, I had only been here a week and he was the first guy that I had gone on a date with. He must've sensed my hesitation. "Do you have anywhere to be this evening?" he said with a cheeky smile. "Nope!" "Ok cool. Let's get dressed, I want to take you to another 'must go to' bar to watch the sunset."

We got lost again walking back to the car. We giggled all the way there and his hand wandered to my waist to guide me in whatever direction he thought was right. He was starting to grow on me. I couldn't remember the last time I had laughed so much with anyone. We hopped in the car where the radio blasted out reggae tunes we giggled and danced to. After a short drive, we pulled into a nearly empty sandy car park. This place was much more my style. It was rustic with overly varnished handmade wooden tables. Garlands of sea shells and starfish hung down from wooden beams on the ceiling. The tables were on the sand, so I kicked off my flip flops and walked as straight as I could towards the table. I was tipsier than I realised. I guess all that car dancing made the alcohol flow quicker through my veins!

"A bottle of your finest rosé please," David said in what was increasingly becoming a sexier English accent. "David! I don't think I can drink another full bottle!" I protested. He laughed and said, "We can always get some nibbles to soak up the alcohol." We carried on getting to know each other, hardly able to tell a story without sarcasm, jokes and giggles. He kept poking my nose with his index finger to get a rise out of me. It was really annoying me, but I knew that's what he wanted, so I laughed it off. Plus, I found it kind of cute. Or maybe it was just the rosé talking...

The sun was hanging above the horizon, so we abandoned our table to watch it dip down into the sea. David sat close enough for our arms to be touching. "It's kind of romantic, isn't it?" He asked. "Oh whatever, you're not getting any," I joked as I jumped up to get in the water. He followed me, "I wouldn't get too close if I were you, I'm peeing!" I exclaimed. "Oooo... the water is a little cold. I like the warm spots," he said as he swam closer to me. I splashed him away, dove under and swam back towards the beach. "Just wait a minute! I can't really get out in public right now," he giggled. "That's pathetic. I didn't even touch you!" I exclaimed. "Yeah, but seeing you wet in that bikini is all I need." "Such a charmer," I said rolling my eyes.

On the drive back to the marina, I realised I didn't want the night to end. I had nothing to do the next day and for the first time in a long time, I was enjoying someone's company. My belly was aching from all the laughs. "Let's go skinny dipping!!" I exclaimed much to the horror of the angel inside of me. Did I really just say that?!?! Shit! That was totally the rosé talking. "Great idea. I like your style," David said as he flashed a flirtatious grin my way. That was it. I said it and he liked the idea, there was no turning back. We drove around a bend and the view of the marina at night filled the windscreen. Little white and red dots of the mast lights scattered the bay. The sailboat spreaders were all lit up boasting their beautiful presence.

The devil inside of me was pleased that we were the only car at the beach. There would be no excuse to renege on my spontaneous idea. I left my flip flops in the car and ran to the beach, stripping off my shirt and swimsuit top as I went. "Hey! Wait for me!" David shouted after me. "No way, hurry up!" I shouted. I quickly ripped off my shorts and bikini bottoms. I ran into the sea screaming like an excited child and dove into the mini waves.

David soon followed and disappeared underneath the water. I was waiting for him to come up for what seemed a little too long. All of the sudden, I felt a nibble at my leg and I screamed. His head popped up and he started laughing. "Thought it was a shark, huh?" "I would be happier if it was," I said as I tried to swim away. He grabbed my foot and pulled me towards him. "Where do you think you're going little lady?" He reached in for a kiss and I surrendered. Wow was I glad that I did. He was a great kisser and I instantly became putty in his hands. I wrapped my legs around his waist and my arms around his neck. "Mmmmm..." I moaned as the kiss became more passionate. "Eeeww! Control yourself man!" I pushed him away as I felt his hard cock pressing up against me. "I'm not that kind of girl. It takes more than one date to get lucky with me." I swam away and enjoyed the sensation of the warm salt water rushing over my naked body. Skinny dipping in the ocean is one of the most sensual and exciting foreplay activities that exists. Oh how I wanted to go home with him, but I still hadn't made my mind up about him. "Right, let's go," I ordered. "So soon? We just got here. Just come here." "Nope, I want to go home now. Maybe another time," I yelled as I swam towards shore.

I got dressed before he came to shore. "What was that all about?" he asked. "Nothing. I wanted to go skinny dipping and I did. Now it's time for bed," I pecked his lips and walked towards the car. "My bed or your bed?" he asked. "You go to your bed and I'll go to mine." "Alright, I guess I'll take you home then." I accepted another caress of his lips before getting out of the car. "Thanks for the fun day. It's been a long time since I've laughed that hard," I said. "The pleasure is mine. We'll have to do it another time and hopefully it will end with us in the same bed," he said with a sparkle in his eye. I walked away, turned around and smiled, "Maybe! Good night."

CHAPTER 60

The sunshine peeked through the lace curtains blowing in the breeze. I opened my eyes and rolled over. Ooofff. I could feel the rosé. I cringed as I remembered the skinny dipping incident. The lack of alcohol gave me some clarity about how my first intuition about David was to stay away. "Oh well," I said as I peeled myself out of bed and into my hiking clothes. It was my last Monday off before starting a new job, so I wanted to take advantage of it. The goat trail was my daily half hour hike, which is up a steepish hill and overlooks the bay at the top. One of the entry points to the trail is at the marina where David's boat is. As I got to the part that overlooked the marina, I stood back in the bushes like a proper stalker to see if he was outside. I saw someone on deck, but it wasn't him. I giggled to myself at how ridiculous I was being and carried on walking.

When I returned home, I picked up my phone and saw a message from David. "Yesterday was fun. Want to come over and watch a movie? I'm on watch." "Sure. As long as you can take me home afterwards." I replied with a smile. Who am I kidding? Cuddling on a sofa watching a movie after a whole day of deep belly laughs and fun? I wouldn't be going home.

I walked to the boat and met the other crew onboard, who were a couple. The four of us sat in the saloon half watching a movie and half getting to know each other. Cameron and Janice were hilarious, which made for a really good vibe. After seeing the guest cabin I would be staying in, I had definitely made my mind up. I was going to stay in luxury tonight! A big comfy bed with air conditioning sounded like a dream after my 30 year old mattress in the hot and sticky weather.

The movie ended and David said, "Right little lady, should I take you home now?" "Or do you want to stay and watch another movie?" asked Janice. "I'm tired so I'm either taking you home now or you can stay and watch a movie and sleep here," David said. I paused, pretending like it was a hard decision, "Ok. I'll stay here." David squeezed me closer and Janice screamed with excitement.

Not long into the movie, David whispered in my ear, "C'mon. Let's go to my cabin." I sat up, said good night to Cameron and Janice and followed David into the box of luxury. "There's an extra toothbrush behind the mirror if you want to brush your teeth," David said. Oh the joys of yachts, all of the toiletries you could possibly imagine at your fingertips. "I didn't bring any pyjamas." He opened up a drawer and took out a fresh, clean boat t-shirt. "You can wear this if you feel you need to wear something," he smirked. I changed into the shirt, took my shorts off and climbed in between the soft Egyptian sheets. "Aaaahhhh, not a bad life I've made for myself," I thought to myself with a smile.

David came out of the head and took off everything but his boxer shorts. I had already noted his muscular body on the beach. What he lacked in height, he made up with muscles. His arms were burly and strong. I tried to hold back fantasies of him picking me up and flipping me over. He crawled into bed, laid on his back and lifted his arm up, "Come on. Come under here." I wasn't going to fight an invitation to cuddle.

I nestled my head on his chest and he wrapped his arm around me. "It's been a while since I've slept on a boat," I commented. "I've really missed it." "Oh yeah?" he replied and without a further word, he tilted my chin up and gave me a kiss. He rolled onto his side and kissed me with more intention. Oooohhh, his kisses. They were soft and gentle, but with direction and confidence. He wasted no time. His free hand found its way up my shirt to play with my nipple. The sensible part of me wanted to protest and the horny side of me shut it down quickly. An involuntary note of pleasure escaped my throat.

David took this as an invitation to keep going. He rolled me onto my back and sat on top of me. He grabbed the bottom of my shirt and lifted it over my head. Without hesitation, I raised my arms so he could more easily complete his mission. He sat up, visually soaking in my naked breasts for a second, before gently diving in for another kiss. He grabbed my hands and held them behind my head as he nibbled at my ears.

A tingle of pleasure ran all through my body. My legs involuntary wrapped themselves around him as if to say, "You're not going anywhere. Don't stop." He lowered his lips to my neck and let go of my hands. I wrapped my arms around him to pull him close, but he leaned back and gave me a sexy dominating look. He took my hands and held them above my head with one hand. I read the command loud and clear. I'm not allowed to touch him.

He made his way down to my clit, stopping briefly to give my nipples some attention. There was no teasing, no kissing around the area, he firmly and quickly started licking my now sopping wet pussy. He was in charge. He instinctively knew my body and what pleasured me. He was a confident lover, which fit with his arrogant engineering personality. It was so attractive and sexy and allowed me to submit to him completely. He hurriedly ripped off his boxer shorts as his tongue gave me so much pleasure, I nearly orgasmed.

David placed my legs on either side of his shoulders and lifted my pelvis towards him. Any doubt I had over the last two days completely disappeared. He reached over to find a condom and put it on with one hand while two fingers of his other hand made their way into my love tunnel. I was impressed with his multi-tasking skills. As soon as the condom was on, he resumed position and his palpitating cock entered me without guidance.

I screamed out and grabbed the sheets with my fists. "Oh you're so deep, that feels so good," I whispered in near ecstasy. He was giving me slow deep thrusts enabling me to feel every part of him. I was so close to climaxing despite the hurried, yet fulfilling foreplay. I begged him to go faster. He again gave me that dominating look informing me who was in command. I immediately submitted and let go of the sheets, allowing any tension in my body to release.

David whipped my legs down and grabbed my arms to pull me up towards him. Now I was the one that was in charge of the rhythm as I sat on his cock. His mouth found its way to my nipples and he sucked hard. I completely let loose, it was so passionate and intense that my hips thrusted quicker back and forth, back and forth and within what seemed like seconds, I came. I grabbed his head pulling it towards my chest as my back arched with satisfaction. He gently bit my nipples intensifying my orgasm.

I had no time to recuperate as I found myself being pushed back onto the bed and David on top of me again. I felt my pleasure zone throbbing as he found his own rhythm. I tried to move my hips and help him along, but my orgasm was so intense that all I had the energy for was offering encouragement through muffled groans of enjoyment. It wasn't long and he came as well.

He exhaustedly laid on top of me. Our bodies out of breath and fully satisfied. After a few minutes lying like that, David rolled over to the side and said, "Glad you stayed?" "Nah, not really. I've had better." I giggled. His arrogance and cockiness were sometimes unattractive, but it allowed me to make sarcastic comments like that. I knew my screams of pleasure throughout the whole sexual adventure told him how I really felt. We fell asleep wrapped in each other's arms as the murmur of the air conditioning cooled our sweaty and gratified bodies.

CHAPTER 61

The next weekend, Janice texted me. "Hey doll. I'm on watch so if you want to stop by and keep me company that would be super. The guys are out." I texted David, "Hey. I'm going to hang out with Janice on the boat today. Should I bring an overnight bag?" "Sounds great," he replied.

I went to the boat just after lunch and Janice offered me a beer. "They are David's, but we can just go to the shops later and restock." After we polished off the last few beers, she suddenly spurted out, "Oh, we have pina coladas! I forgot I made them the other day and there was some leftover. Do you want one of those?" she asked. "Of course! We're in the Caribbean." We went to the galley and chatted nonstop. Janice decided there wasn't enough mix so she made more. The blender jug became fuller and fuller as she insisted on getting the perfect balance of each ingredient.

Not surprisingly, the afternoon turned quite messy. We decided to have a dance party in the cockpit. The sun was shining brightly, the music was blaring, we were well lit up and our best dance moves were on display. After all, it was just the two of us, there was no one else to judge us. David and Cameron stumbled on to the boat just before sunset. David rejected the pina coladas claiming he had some important work task in the morning, but he joined us in the cockpit as the three of us finished off the remaining pina colada mix.

Cameron, being a chef, suggested that we all get some food in us to soak up the alcohol. Janice and I were much more lubricated than the guys were. After we ate, David said, "I'm tired. I'm going to watch a move in my cabin. Want to come?" "Don't be so boring David!" Janice exclaimed. "Yeah, I don't want to watch a movie, let's dance!" David, having sobered up said, "You dance. I'm going to watch a movie, come into the cabin when you're done."

We didn't want to carry on disturbing the neighbouring yachts, so we took the dance party inside. Cameron and Janice's cabin was right across from David's in the guest area. They were located at the start of a long corridor which led to the master cabin. Cameron was in charge of the play list and started playing disco. In order to make this a proper party, a disco ball was required. Cameron drunkenly downloaded a bunch of disco ball apps, none of which met our standards. After admitting defeat, Cameron went into his cabin to take a shower.

"Hold on a second," Janice said to me. She left me standing alone in the corridor. I opened up David's cabin door to see what he was up to. "Are you sleeping?" I asked. "How the fuck can I sleep when there's loud music and giggling outside of my door." "Alright Mr Grumpy," I said flirtatiously as I jumped onto the bed. "Are you coming to bed now?" he asked with a smile. "Nope," Cameron is taking a shower and Janice went to do something, so I thought I would say hi." I straddled him and gave him a kiss. "I think you should come to bed now," he said pulling me closer to him. I pushed myself back. There was a loud knock on the door, "Brizo!! Come out! I want to show you something! Or can I come in? Is David naked? If I open the door, will I see his cock? I want to see his cock, but I don't want to," she giggled. "I better go," I said jumping off the bed.

I opened up the door, "Follow me," Janice said with a mischievous look in her eye. I sauntered into their cabin and went with her to the bathroom door. "I want to share something with you," she said. One thing I forgot to note was that all of the guest heads had glass shower doors. She slowly opened up the door, "Look! There he is, that's my Cameron!" she proudly exclaimed. "Janice! What are you doing? Are you pimping me out again?" Cameron replied. I was laughing so hard I could barely speak. "She's not doing a very good job because the glass is all fogged up and I can't see anything!" "Oh. Well let me fix that," Cameron stated. He wiped away the fog from his nether regions and Janice and I started screaming with laughter. "Ok girls! That's enough," Cameron announced.

We barrelled back into the bedroom in fits of giggles. "Oh my god!! I have the perfect song for when Cameron comes out," Janice exclaimed. "Wait for it." We left the cabin to give Cameron some privacy and carried on dancing in the corridor. The door to David's cabin opened, "Can you turn the music down?" We both looked at him with disgust. "No, sorry!" and I shut the door on him. Janice checked to see if Cameron was out of the shower. He was in his boxer shorts, buttoning up his shirt. "Cameron! I'm going to play the best song!" Janice shouted. "I'm too sexy for my shirt.. too sexy for my shirt.. so sexy it hurts." Cameron's face turned serious and he slowly unbuttoned his shirt. .

"Let's go on the catwalk!" Janice screamed. The corridor was a perfect runway for us to show off our sexiest moves. We took turns and as the song ended, David burst into the corridor. "Alright that's enough. It's getting late now. Get in here right now Brizo." Janice and I rolled our eyes. "When did you turn into such a grandpa?" I asked. He muttered something about having to work the next day and pulled me by the arm into his cabin. "Good night!" I shouted back at Brizo and Cameron as the door closed.

"Am I going to get punished for being a bad girl?" I asked with a sparkle in my eye. "Yes, you're not getting any," he said. "Oh whatever, I'll believe it when I see it," I slurred. I asked him if I could take a shower. "You're more than welcome to join me." "Fuck that, I'm tired. But leave the door open so I can watch."

I stepped out of the shower and dried off in the sexiest manner my drunken state could muster. I hung my towel on the hook and crawled from the bottom of the bed up to his head. I tried to give him a kiss. "I told you, you're not getting any," he said as he rejected my kiss. "Ok." I moved the sheet down his chest, kissing it as I went down. What guy rejects a blow job? I knew he was just playing hard to get.

I teased him by kissing his inner thighs and gently stroking his growing cock with my hand. As he became hard and firm, I circled the tip of his penis with my tongue before taking him fully into my mouth. I started off slow and adjusted the rhythm of my strokes and mouth moving up and down to the growing sounds of his pleasure. "Where are the condoms?" I asked. "We used the last one the other day." "Well it's your lucky day then," I said as I took his mast back into my mouth. I sucked harder, moving my hand faster up and down until my mouth filled with his salty seawater. I looked up at him and swallowed. "How was that?" "Fuck," was his only response. He pulled me up towards him and kissed me on the lips. "I

suppose it's your turn now." "Nah," I replied. "I'm all good."
"Are you sure?" he asked. "Absolutely," I said as I nestled my
head into his chest.

CHAPTER 62

The next morning, I awoke to David spooning me. I felt his arm reach around me and his finger made its way to my clit. "Good morning," I muttered. "Shhh.." David said. It didn't take long for the moistness to creep into my loins. When I was sufficiently saturated, he pushed his hard cock into me. He shoved me forward to have a better angle and slowly started sliding in and out. My head was slightly sore, so I was glad I didn't have to play an active role. He placed my hand onto my clit as an invitation to play with myself. My moistness increased as he sped up. He pulled out and kissed the back of my neck. "That was naughty," he referred to not using a condom. "I have to get up for work, but you can lie here as long as you like." I rolled over to give him a kiss. He gently kissed each of my nipples before getting dressed. After he left, I laid naked on the bed wondering if I should pleasure myself or wait until the next time. I opted to wait.

I dressed for my routine morning hike. I packed up my bag and said see you later to David, Janice and Cameron. During my hike and swim, I replayed the evening in my mind. I felt alive and refreshed after a night of fun and light-heartedness. David told me he wasn't looking for anything serious, which was perfect. I dipped in the tepid salty sea with a big smile on my face.

When I got home, I was abruptly forced back to reality when a text from Adonis popped up, "Hey. I have a surprise for you," followed by a photo of flight details saying that he was coming to the island in two days. "Shit."

David sent me a photo with the caption "You left these here." He was wearing my cut off jean shorts and had a goofy smile on his face. Upon closer inspection, his dick was hanging out the bottom of one of the legs. "Come and get them." Oh god, he makes me laugh so hard!! "My ex is coming in two days," I replied. "What?? For real! I guess we don't have much more time for fun then," he replied. "I'll stop by later and pick up my shorts," I wrote. I was disappointed our time was ending so abruptly. Of course, it was romantic that Adonis was flying over to try and win me back, but surely, we should've talked about this before he booked a ticket???

The day before Adonis came, I went over to pick up my shorts. I made sure Janice would be there as well so that I wouldn't be alone with David. I wasn't sure if my pants would stay up if he started to make me laugh. He had just returned from the gym. "Wait in my cabin while I shower," he told me. Ever the exhibitionist, he left the head door open so I could watch him in full glory. We chatted about our days and how I was feeling about Adonis coming.

He came out of the shower and lifted my skirt up. "Why are you wearing underwear?" he asked. "David, come on. Adonis is coming tomorrow. I don't want to fuck you again before he comes. I'm sorry." He tried his luck one more time before exclaiming, "I'm sad we don't get to play together more. I was looking forward to throwing you around more and exploring." "I know, I would've liked that too, but I owe it to Adonis to hear him out. But if it doesn't work out between him and I, I will gladly accept your invitation," I remarked.

I got up, took my shorts and said, "Thanks for a really fun week. I haven't had those laughs in a long time. I'm going to miss you." He came over for a hug and I engaged in one last kiss before Adonis, ever the troubadour, flew in to try and salvage our love story.

ADONIS RETURNS

CHAPTER 63

I was living on the boat where I started working earlier in the week, so I booked a hotel room for two nights with Adonis. I had such mixed feelings about him. The hotel was in Nelson's Dockyard close to the boat. Adonis wasn't getting in until the evening, so Janice and I went to check in and look at the room. It was so nice! They offered us a welcome drink and I told Janice to take Adonis' as I didn't think he would mind. It was a big suite with two floors and three beds. A big playground for Adonis and I to reacquaint ourselves on. "Are you going to tell Adonis about David?" Janice asked as we sipped on our welcome rum punches. "No, I don't think there's a point. We were broken up and it will only hurt him." I justified.

At last, the butterflies could stop swirling around in my belly. I was waiting in reception for Adonis' arrival. I saw the taxi door open and Adonis stepped out. Janice and I had carried on drinking, so I was happily tipsy and very excited to see him. He gave me a huge squeeze and a long passionate kiss. The familiarity of his touch and energy sent shivers down my spine and into my groin. He looked deeply into my eyes and said, "God, I missed you." "I missed you too," I replied. We went up to the room and Adonis barely had time to put his bag down before I was all over him. His touch was so comfortable and well known to me, I wanted more than just that passionate kiss. I helped him undress. I was wearing his favourite blue flowered dress to make for easy access. I had taken my underwear off before I went downstairs to wait for him. There was no use in wasting time having to remove them.

Adonis lifted me up. I wrapped my legs around him as he carried me over to the nearest bed. He laid me down gently as we gazed into each other's eyes. All of my love for him flooded back and an enormous wave of guilt smacked me in the face. I knew if he ever found out about David, he would be destroyed. I parked that thought in the back of my drunken mind as he carried out his expert engineering maintenance on my body. My whole body melted into the soft mattress as his tongue re-familiarised itself with my pussy. "Mmmm...I forgot how good you tasted," he mumbled. "I didn't even realise how much I missed this," he said while looking up at me. "I love you," he whispered before diving in for some more juice. "Oooooooohhhh...you feel so good," I said. "I missed that for sure."

"Fuck me Adonis," I commanded. "Wait, I'm not done here," he said. "I want to feel you inside of me," I replied. "I want you to fuck me hard." He carried on licking me for a couple of minutes before sliding his tongue up my torso, chest, biting each nipple as he went and stopping to stare in my eyes. "I love you so much Brizo. I'm so sorry everything turned it out the way it did." "Shhh..." I said with a smile. "You're here now." I found his pleasure wand and guided it inside of me. "Jesus you're so wet," he responded.

Our bodies found their old rhythm like two long lost dance partners. He wrapped his arms around me and carried me with him as he laid down on his back so that I was straddling him. "I want to look at how beautiful you are," he said. Our hips became still as he ran his hands over my breasts, my sides and my tummy. "I love your tummy," he said squeezing the pocket of fat I've always hated.

I slowly started moving my hips back and forth. He closed his eyes and I felt electric sensations of pleasure running from his throbbing cock up into my pussy and through me. My movement gradually became quicker as I became more and more aroused. I stuck my chest out and threw my head back. He played with my clit and the state of deep relaxation I was in brought on an unexpected orgasm. Adonis not having had a release in much longer than me, let go and came with me. His eyes turned into the back of his head, he groaned and his body jerked as the pleasure escaped from the tip of his penis.

"Wow. That was intense!" I said lovingly. I didn't move. His softening cock was still pulsing in my vagina and I squeezed my pelvic floor muscles to prolong his pleasure. I don't normally regret my actions, but I sensed a renewed love coming from Adonis and I was annoyed with myself for jumping on to someone else so quickly.

I worked the next day and he met me at the boat to meet my crew and have a drink. The two of us went for a romantic dinner. I was dealing with my guilt by drinking quickly. Adonis made a comment about my drinking, which I fobbed off by saying, "It's the Caribbean, that's what we're supposed to do!" On the way home, we stopped at one of the bars and danced to the live music. We were that annoying couple who grinded and kissed on the dance floor. "Come on, we better get going. Remember you have to work in the morning," Adonis said. I'm sure he said it out of love, but it rubbed me the wrong way. "Ok, Dad!" I snapped.

I grabbed his hand and we left. "What's going on with you Brizo?" he asked. "I'm tired and I want to make love to you before we snuggle for the evening." I was on full defence. "Maybe you should've said that instead of acting like a parent," I shouted. "Jesus, you need to watch your drinking if it's going to make you violent." "Violent? Fuck you! It has nothing to do with the alcohol. I fucked some guy since I've been here and I feel terrible." He stopped dead in his tracks. "You what?" "You heard me. I don't need to say it again," I said. I turned around and his shoulders were slumped, his head was hanging down and he was rubbing his forehead. "I can't fucking believe it."

We went back to our hotel room where he laid on his side on the bed and cried. The alcohol mixed with guilt was making me cold. I didn't feel like I could console him. "I'm so sorry," I said. "Why did you do it?" he asked. "Adonis, we broke up. I was spending time with someone who made me laugh and I think you can agree it's been a long time since we've made each other laugh." He cried harder. "I'm sorry," he said. "No, I'm sorry," I replied. I snuggled up to him, wrapped my arm around him and gave him a big hug. I felt his body jerking from silent sobs. The next thing I remember is my alarm going off. When I turned around to say good morning to Adonis, he was scrolling through his phone. "Good morning," I said. "Hey," he replied shortly. "Did you get any sleep?" I asked. "Nope." "Babe, I'm so sorry, I'm also really sorry that I have to go to work." "Yeah," he replied.

The work day seemed to last years. I was so worried about Adonis and just wanted to get back to him to see how he was. Finally, the day ended and I could rush off. He was in the same position as when I left him. "Are you ok?" I asked. "No," he replied firmly. I tried talking to him, but he was barely responding. Finally, I gave up. "I have to take a shower. I stink," I said. I rolled off the bed and hopped in the shower. As I was rinsing the shampoo out of my hair, I heard the shower curtain being pulled open.

I opened one eye and Adonis was naked coming into the shower with me. He spun me around and shoved my hips towards him while pushing my back down. My head was up against the shower wall and he forcefully thrust in and out of me. He noticed that I was being pushed up against the wall, so he grabbed my chest and pulled me to standing position. He then pushed me against the wall and fucked me hard. My face was smashed against the shower wall, but I didn't care. Adonis wasn't normally so passionately aggressive, which is something I had always asked for. He came inside of me, rinsed his cock off and left. Not one word was spoken this whole time. I finished showering and walked to the bed naked.

"Fuck that was hot," I said in disbelief. Adonis shrugged his shoulders. "That's what I always wanted from you," I replied sitting down next to him. "I guess I just have to be destroyed to have angry sex." "Well did you like it?" I asked ignoring the guilt that was searing through my body. "Yeah, it wasn't bad. You?" he said half smiling. "It was fucking hot, but I haven't finished yet," I winked. "Then sort yourself out," he said. I laid next to him, "Can you help me please?" I fingered my clit while he sucked on my nipples. The intensity of the shower fuck was so high that it didn't take me long. He bit my nipple harder, sending me into an overwhelming state of arousal and I orgasmed, screaming loudly with the release.

After a week of trying to make it work, Adonis decided to leave when he got a job offer in St Martin.

ARNO

CHAPTER 64

"Hey Brizo!" Arno said loudly. I walked under the hatch, squeezing my boobs together along the way, "Yeessss Arno?" "Nothing! Just needed to see that. Thanks!" The hatch slid shut behind him, taking away the intense heat of the day along with the sight of Arno's beaming bright smile. It was a little joke between him and I. The crew entrance is a three meter climb up a ladder attached to the wall of the interior. The hatch slides open and closed and the deck crew often pass power leads, coffee cups or guest towels down the hatch.

After a week of being onboard, Arno admitted that he enjoyed when I was the one that answered his calls because he saw my cleavage when he looked down. He was in his mid-twenties, I wasn't going to deprive him of his sexual needs. He was already working 24-7, which made it impossible for him to get off the boat to find a little fun. After his confession of wanting me at first sight, I decided to have a little fun and accentuate my cleavage. He said it made his day. I'm in the business of making people happy.

Arno was tall, of stocky build with black hair and innocent dark brown eyes that sparkled when he talked. He had a baby face with a thick moustache hiding his top lip. Kindness and care radiated from his easy and frequent smile. He was a cutie, but not my type. I really enjoyed being in his presence and soaking in his youthful positive energy. His optimism was unbeatable and it was hard for me to stay in my permanent bad mood when we talked.

Arno made it clear early on that he had a thing for me. Or rather should I say, one of his very helpful crew mates made sure I knew of this little crush. I loved flirting with Arnos and sometimes I could see how much he was enjoying it because he would have to wait on a deck a little longer before going to help a guest. When I discovered this little fact, I made it even more of a game to see how frequently I could pull up his sail.

"Hey Arno," I said in my sexiest voice. "How's it going up here on deck?" I said deck in a way that was hard to determine if I said deck or dick. I walked as close to him as I could without the guests suspecting something was happening between us. I offered to help him with what he was doing and made sure some part of me was touching him. I saw something lying on the deck and bent over from the hips to give him a clear view of my ass. "Oh my god, thank you, thank you!" he replied shaking his hands in a prayer gesture up at the sky. To say the least, it was very flattering having someone 15 years younger than me melting at the sight of me. Win/win situation if you ask me.

I was freelancing on the boat for five weeks with the possibility of an extension, but I had already made up my mind up that I wasn't extending if they asked. Despite the fun little games Arno and I had, I didn't gel with the rest of the crew and things were pretty tough at times. Arno was very sweet in noticing this. I started to meet him at the bow when he was alone having a cigarette break.

"It must be really tough being on a boat with people you don't have anything in common with. It's not like you can get off in the evening and see friends," he empathised. "I know, it's really hard and I haven't been off the boat in like ten days. I just want to get out of here for like half an hour to have some time to myself without someone asking me for something or talking to me. I'm slowly losing my mind," I replied. "Well, the guests are having dinner onshore tonight so maybe we can go for a swim. I know it's not the same as being on land, but if it's just the two of us, then it won't be so bad, right?" he said with a cheeky grin. I've been around boats and sailors long enough to know that this is an opportunity to have a little feel! "That would be lovely. Thank you," I smiled back at him. We were anchored off an island near the Italian coast.

"You know there are sharks in these waters, right? It's a breeding ground for sharks," the other stewardess informed us. "Oh whatever. Even if it is a breeding ground, they won't be dangerous sharks. We're in the Med," I retorted. "It's great whites!" she exclaimed. Arno and I laughed and carried on stripping down to our swim gear. I jumped in first and he followed. "Oh this is amazing!!" I exclaimed. "I love night swimming. Even better skinny dipping, but hey ho," I flirted. "We can skinny dip. It's dark!" he said all too eagerly. "They'll take our clothes and towels from us, I'm not in the mood for that." I started swimming away and Arno called me back. "Do you think there are sharks in here for real?" he asked. "No, I don't think so. They wouldn't be happy here." "Ok, but let's not go too far just in case." I laughed, "Good idea." I had to admit, I was a little freaked out by the idea.

We both swam out of sight of the crew's curious eyes. Everyone saw our outrageous flirting, so they would be expecting something to happen. "Come closer," he whispered coyly. I did as asked, and he grabbed my waist. I wrapped my arms around him, "That's better," he said. I giggled as the weight of me made it hard for him to keep his head above the water. We were in a rocky anchorage with an annoying swell. I laid back so that my full weight wasn't on him, "Hmmm...I wish I could get a clearer view of that, but from what I can see, that's so sexy." "It's the only time my boobs are perky," I laughed. "There ain't nothing wrong with those boobies!" he replied. "Do you think we should kiss?" he asked, showing his inexperience with women. I unwrapped my legs from him and shook my head while smiling, "I don't think so Arno. You're the first mate, that isn't very professional." "Well, it never hurts to ask," he said. He came from a protective upbringing and had already admitted to me that despite having a few long-term relationships, he still had a lot to learn when it came to the female realm.

"I'll get out first," I said. Sharks or no sharks, the idea of not being able to see what's underneath me always creeps me out at night. Usually, I have to be drunk before I jump in the water after the sun sets. "You're going to have to! If the other guys are on deck, I can't get out right now," he squeaked. I couldn't resist. I reached over and had a feel of his groin. "Well that isn't going to help is it???" he shouted. "Whatever you do, just don't look at my ass as I get out of the water," I giggled. I slowly climbed up the ladder, sticking my bum out so he would have an unobscured view. "Oh Jesus. This isn't fucking fair!" he shouted in a whisper. I laughed and rinsed myself off with fresh water.

"So did anything happen in the water?" asked the nosey stew. "No, we just went swimming. It felt good to be off the boat, even if I was still near it." "Are you going to sleep with him? I think you should sleep with him," she egged on. I rolled my eyes, "He's so much younger than me. Not happening." I really wasn't interested in having girl talk with someone who was one of the biggest gossips I had met in a long time. Besides, I was used to being with much more experienced men and wasn't interested in engaging in a teaching role after what happened with Jeremy.

CHAPTER 65

After a particularly difficult working day, I noticed that everyone but Arno was in the crew mess. I checked on the guests, who said they were wrapping up to go to bed and I was no longer needed. I crept up to the bow and found Arno smoking. "Hey sexy!" he said with that award winning smile. Probably the first genuine smile of the night creeped up on my face. "You're so sweet Arno," I replied.

"How's it going?" he asked. "Not such a good day. I just want to get off of this boat and go home," I said with tears in my eyes. "Aww come on, it can't be that bad. I'm glad you're onboard." Tears welled up in my eyes, "Thanks Arno. That's really kind of you to say." "Come here for a hug," he said. He gave me a big squeeze that made me feel so much better. I sat cross legged close to him. He started circling his finger on my knee. "Hey, watch it!," I smirked. "What? I'm not doing anything wrong," he said as his finger went higher up my thigh. "Damn these shorts!!! Do they make them tight so pervy deck crew can't get their fingers up them??" "That's exactly the reason," I blurted with laughter.

I moved my leg to try and loosen the shorts, but he could only go up a few centimetres more. "Damn. Well, I'm hoping once the guests leave that I'll be able to get these shorts off." I rolled my eyes, "You're so cute. Thanks for making me laugh."

Arno gave up trying to go under the leg of my shorts and instead rubbed his hand on the outside of my crotch. I looked at him and lifted an eyebrow. "Should I stop?" he asked. "I don't know," I replied with genuine confusion. "Well that isn't a no." "Mmmm...that feels really nice," I moaned. "I wish the guests weren't onboard right now. It would make my life a lot easier," he said. I dropped my head back to look at the stars while enjoying the hands of a guy 15 years my junior eagerly wanting to feel my body. "I better see if the guests are in bed so I can clean up and go to bed," I remarked. "Ahh, ok. If you have to," he said with disappointment. I stood up, gave him a hug and kissed his forehead, "Good night. Sleep tight," I whispered as I walked away.

CHAPTER 66

"Brizo! Go up to the bow. Arno always fucks up when you're there and he needs to learn to keep his focus no matter what's going on," the captain said as I walked up to the helm station. We were picking up anchor and heading over to the stunning Amalfi coast. "Challenge accepted," I announced confidently as I walked to the bow.

"Hey Arno," I said flirtatiously. "Nooooo... don't come up here! I can't concentrate when you're here." "I know. The good old captain told me you need to learn to focus." "Mother fucker," he replied. Everyone knows that a captain's orders need to be followed, so I did my best to distract him.

I leaned over with the perfect agle so he wouldn't be able to resist looking down my shirt. Then I bent over the other way so he could see my ass. "Brizo!!! You're really not helping!" he shouted nervously. "Oh, sorry. I was just helping you clean up the deck," I teased. "So I was thinking about your wandering hands last night..." I said. "Not now Brizo! Arrggghh!! Just go away!" he shouted in frustration. I laughed. I didn't leave, but I stopped teasing him. When he pulled up and secured the anchor, I muttered, "Well, my work here is done!" and I paraded off to the helm station towards a laughing captain.

For the next few days, the conversations we could sneak in when alone at the bow turned sexual in nature. Arno divulged that the only women he slept with were his limited number of serious girlfriends. "I'm sure you could teach me a thing or two," he remarked hopefully. "I'm sure I could Arno. I have 15 years experience on you," I said with a laugh. "I would be an eager student," he pressed. "Arno, come on. It is physically possible that I could be your mother." "Yeah, you're a MILF!" I giggled, "Whatever. Keep wishing," I said.

The guests were out for dinner and us crew were in the stern lying on the deck smoking. As usual, the conversation turned to sex. That's what happens when a horny crew are deprived of it. The captain asked Arno, "You've been on the boat for years now. How many girls have you fucked in the master cabin?" "None," Arno said sheepishly. "But that's because the previous captain wouldn't allow us to sleep in the guest cabins." "What?!?! Well, I'm not that kind of captain. Fuck whoever you want in there. Maybe Brizo will be up for it. Right, Brizo?" he said. "Mario, don't put ideas in his head. He's only a kid." I retorted. "Exactly, he needs an older woman to show him the ropes." I felt the sexual tension between Arno and I growing. "It's only a matter of time," I thought to myself.

CHAPTER 67

At last!! Drop off day arrived! It doesn't matter how nice the guests are, working on a yacht is a 24-7 hour job for as long as they are onboard. I was happy to have some freedom back and it also meant that I would be going home soon to my friends. The other stewardess and I organised the interior and joined the engineer, chef and captain on deck for some drinks. "Where's Arno?" I enquired. "Probably in the master cabin waiting naked for you," joked the captain. "Mario. Get over it!" "Come on, you should just make the guy's dreams come true," he said. "Where is he really?" I asked. "He's up at the bow, he has to do a washdown before he can have a drink." "Alright, I'll go help him," I replied.

"You don't have to help me. Go and enjoy a drink with the rest of the crew," Arno said as I grabbed a soapy sponge out of the bucket. "That's alright. It's not fair one person is working and the rest aren't. Plus, you're my favourite crew member, so I would rather hang out with you." When he walked away to do something else, I grabbed the hose to rinse off the section I was working on. He walked back towards me and I 'accidentally' sprayed him with the hose. It's cheesy, but never gets old! He stood there laughing, "Watch it you. I'll get you back later," he said. "I hope I get sprayed with a hose soon!" I teased.

We finished and joined the others for a well deserved drink or 20. The lack of sleep and amount of hours we work can only be rewarded by a piss up. Arno and I sat next to each other at the end of the table. The famous talker of the group was talking away about himself and other things I had either heard before or wasn't interested in. The rest of the crew were listening intently. I drank quicker to deal with the boredom.

Janice and Cameron were arriving tomorrow to replace myself and the chef, so I just had to get through tonight and tomorrow before being in the company of good friends. Arno was acting like such a sweetheart. When I stood up to get more drinks, he pushed down on my shoulder and said, "I got this. You've done enough service the last two weeks." He was filling my yearning to be taken care of. The alcohol flowed faster between my lips and my resolve not to spread my legs for him was quickly weakening.

"Right, I'm going to have a shower before I drink too much," declared Arno. "Good idea," I said and followed him inside. No one at the table had taken note of this little exchange as they were all too enthralled in the story being told. When we got into the crew mess I said, "Grab a towel and your soap and meet me in the VIP cabin." "What??? We can't shower in there," he said. "Mario gave us permission and I'm the stewardess. We'll just clean up after ourselves and no one will know." I replied.

We met in the cabin and undressed to shower. "Is this really happening?" Arno said with amazement. "Turn around, let me wash your back," I ordered. "Oh my god, she's even washing my back. This is amazing!" he said to no one in particular. As he turned around to rinse his back off, I gently played with his penis using my soapy hand. "This guy may be getting some use tonight. We have to make sure he's looking his best," I said flirtatiously. "Oh my god, I really hope so!" he remarked.

I went down on my knees and gently pushed him back so that the water ran down to rinse off his quickly growing cock. When it was soap free, I licked the tip of his penis and gently placed my hand under his balls. "Oh my god, is this really happening?" he said in awe. I licked up and down his shaft and took his whole pole inside of my mouth. "Oh my god. I think I'm going to come in like 3 seconds," he said as he pressed his back against the shower wall. I used my hand and mouth in unison to ensure he reached climax. As he came, I pulled my mouth away and carried on with my hand. "Wow. This must be what heaven feels like," he exclaimed. "Good," I said as I started to wash myself. "Can I help you?" he asked. "You can wash my back if you want," I said. His hands went gently up and down my back and slipped down to my bum. "Mmmm...I want to do things to you," he said. I turned around and said, "This is just a warm up. Not yet." I finished washing myself as he towelled off. "I'll meet you on deck after I chamois the shower," I informed him. "I'll do that, you're probably sick of it by now." "Totally! I won't argue you with you there!" I replied. We got dressed and slipped back into our seats on deck.

"Where were you two?" asked one of the crew. "I was on the phone," I replied. "I took a shower," said Arno. "Hmmm...sure..." and he was distracted by the offer of another drink. Arno gave me a secret grin and squeezed my knee.

The night went by in a blur. I was desperate for a break from the boat and the people I had shared it with for the last four weeks. After quite a few more drinks, I said to Arno, "Should we go to bed?" He didn't even respond, he just stood up and walked toward the companionway. I waited a bit and then followed him. He was in the VIP cabin waiting for me. "First let's put a cover on the bed so I don't have to change the sheets again," I said pragmatically. He was like so obedient and immediately helped me lay the cover on the bed. We fumbled around drunkenly taking off some of our clothes before lying down on the bed. I didn't hold any expectations about the sexual adventure I had decided to undertake given his confession of lack of experience.

With some difficulty, Arno unhooked my bra. "Why do they make these things so difficult to take off!" he yelled in frustration. I laughed, "Do you want some help?" He finally succeeded and ripped it off of me, throwing it on the ground.

He circled my nipple gently with his tongue, while rubbing his finger on the tip of my other one. "Well, it's starting off better than anticipated," I thought to myself. I was expecting an awkward fumble with little to no foreplay before quickly heading in to score a goal. His lips found their way down my belly and kept going and going, down one leg all the way to my ankle and up the other side. His touch and soft kisses felt so good. Just like his personality, he was loving and gentle.

After all the stress of the last four weeks, this was just what I needed to release and let go. I relaxed and surrendered to his touch. He found his way to my precious jewel. This must've been his expertise with his ex-girlfriends because he was very confident in what he was doing. It felt amazing. His tongue firmly stroked me up and down as my excitement overflowed. I moaned loudly. He had mentioned that he loved to lick pussy, but I didn't foresee him to be good at it. He used the point of his tongue to flick my clit. I felt myself getting wetter and wetter as my arousal grew. "I'm about to come, please stop." I pleaded. He looked up at me, "Why? You should just come." "Just listen to me!" I said breathless. He gave my pussy one last firm stroke with his tongue before kissing his way back up to my nipples.

"Do me from behind," I ordered. "I can't. My anatomy isn't the right size for that." "Bullshit, everyone can do it. You just have to get the angle right," I said as I pushed him off of me and turned around to all fours. I leant down on my elbows to change the angle and allow him easier access. With only a little difficulty, he found his way inside of me and exclaimed, "Oh my god, I did it!" and smacked my bum before grabbing my hips with both of his hands.

He slowly thrusted deep inside of me. "This feels amazing. I don't want to go too fast or I'll come too quickly," he said. I put my hand on my clit and started playing with myself. His rhythm went faster and faster and I was about to orgasm when he suddenly pulled out. "Sorry, sorry, sorry. I was just about to come." "Just go for it," I said. "You're young, I'm sure you have a good recovery time." Without protest, he slid himself inside of me again and thrusted hard and fast. I tried to make myself come, but the pause in rhythm disturbed my flow. He groaned and gave one last deep thrust. I felt his body jerking. "Did you just come?" I asked. "Yeah, you told me to." "Well I was expecting a warning so I could come too!" I replied disappointingly. "Shit, I know, but that was so hot," he said breathlessly. He held onto my hips, "I can't believe I've never done that before. That felt so good. I want to do it a lot more."

"Did you come?" he asked. "Nope, next round," I winked at him. We laid there for a few moments while he caught his breath. "I've never done it with a girl on top," he admitted. "Really?" I said with astonishment. "That's my favourite position because I can make myself come every time." "Give me 10 minutes and we'll do it," he said as he reached his hand over to play with me again. "Such a gentlemen," I said lying back. I relaxed to his finger discovering the rhythm that made my juices flow again.

After a few minutes, I reached over to inspect his mast. It was semi hard, so I played with it gently, just tickling him with my fingers. As he grew, my strokes became firmer and firmer until he was hard enough to sit on. I climbed on top of him and stuck the tip of him inside me. He tried to push my hips down, "Not yet," I said. "I want to enjoy this game a little bit longer." I moved up and down on the end of his dick, but it had been over a month since I had an orgasm, so I couldn't hold back much longer.

He slowly went all the way into my tunnel with ease. I moved my hips in slow circles as he gave commentary on how all of this was new to him and "amazing." Eventually I lowered my chest to his, rubbing my clit on the tiny bump on his belly, enhancing my excitement. I was on the edge of climax. I sat upright, moving my hips forward to get the right angle. "I'm about to come," I breathed excitedly. His fingers found their way to my nipples and one month of sexual tension exploded out of me. I screamed out in gratification as my body trembled with the release. His hands slid down to my hips and he moved me back and forth to his rhythm. He grunted and pushed me off of him as he had his second orgasm of the evening. I gently slid off to lie next to him, careful not to disturb his freshly emitted seed. I waited for him to catch his breath.

"This is the best night of my life!" He exclaimed. "I had sex with a super hot girl, in the owner's cabin and did two positions I've never done before in my life. I can't believe this has happened." "Glad I could help," I chuckled. With all the alcohol and the physical exhaustion of my intense satisfaction, I quickly fell asleep curled up against him.

CHAPTER 68

I woke up with a start, confused as to where I was. I reached over for my phone to see what time it was and realised where I was. "Shit!" I shouted. "We fell asleep, I have to go back to my cabin," "Why?" he murmured sleepily. "Mario said we could sleep here. Just stay here in my arms," "No, I have to go," I said in a puzzled sleepy stupor. I put my clothes on and snuck to my cabin, surprised to find it empty. My cabinmate must've found a guest cabin to sleep in. "Fuck," I said to myself. The cabin walls hold back no sound. With her loud mouth, everyone would know what happened.

A few hours later, I was awoken by my cabinmate bursting into our cabin. "Oh, I'm surprised to see you here. I could hear what was going on last night and I was like, "Go Arno!" Was it good?" the Queen of gossip enquired. I smiled and rolled over, "A lady never tells."

We didn't have to start work until nine that morning, so I tried to sleep for another hour without much luck. I eventually got up and went out to see where Arno was. He was alone on the dock having a cigarette. "Good morning sexy," he said with that big smile. I was hungover and not feeling as happy as he was. "Sorry, I was so confused when I woke up this morning. Sorry I ran out on you!" I said as I gave him a hug and a playful pat on his ass.

CHAPTER 69

Cameron and Janice arrived a couple of days later. I was happy to see familiar faces and to hand my job off to someone else. When we were having a drink alone in the bar, I told them how I succumbed to the wishes of young Arno. They laughed, "Not at all surprised. He seems like a sweetie and not bad looking either!" "He is, but I'm ready for someone with more sexual experience," I admitted.

I flew back to Mallorca to rest and wait for my next conquest. "Although it's been a lot of fun and I've enjoyed my adventures with much younger men, I'm ready for something different," I thought to myself as the plane took off.

A couple of days later, Janice texted me. "Arno was so sad that you left and everyone made fun of him for how in love he is with you." "Oh no!" I exclaimed. I felt guilty he was upset, but thought texting him would only make the sadness prolonged, so I stayed quiet. This was the exact reason that I was done with younger men, or was I....

ACKNOWLEDGMENTS

It took much internal deliberation to publish this book. No doubt I will be judged and name called, but I'm tired of men having all the fun and glorified for it, while women are still ostracised for the same sexual behaviour. Sex is fun for both men and women, neither should be called names as it's a natural part of life, and quite frankly FUN! It's time to give women the power too.

Some humans are lucky to have found one partner they get to sleep with their whole life and others, like me, are lucky to explore the world of sexuality with many. Whilst all of these deliberations were going on in my head, I was very lucky to have amazing friends who listened and encouraged me to publish it, to name a few Becky, Katie, Darielle, Howard and Luke. If it wasn't for those pushes and talks, years of work may have remained forever locked in my laptop.

Having said this, some people may wonder why I have written under a pseudonym. I am not adverse to putting my real name to this book, that will come when the time is right.

This story wouldn't be possible if I was never taught how to sail, so my biggest thanks to the man who showed me a whole world I didn't even know existed.

At the end of the pandemic, when things weren't quite yet back to normal as far as movements, I decided to take three months off and live in a jungle hut in Nicaragua to write this story. After walking to the beach for sunrise and a bit of meditation, I would climb back up the mountain to write until sunset. The evenings were lonely until I met the lovely Darielle who is herself a writer. We took sunset walks along the beach and had deep and meaningful chats. When I allowed time off from writing, we went on adventures and out for meals. She was inspirational to me and having those chats in the evenings helped keep me focused and sane. Thanks babe.

Which leads me to the next group of people in Nicaragua to thank. By chance I came across a Facebook post about a writer's group. I was a bit wary of how my content would be received, so I went to observe for the first couple of meet ups and then opened up. A big thanks to Gina and Luke for their great feedback and sharing their writing to help give me ideas of new writing styles. A special thanks to Jason who was also in the group and sadly passed away. I hope he reads this and approves from the other side. The look on his face when I finally read out loud a sexual excerpt will forever remain in my memory and give me a smile.

It took me four years to edit this book. I got busy with work, I lost interest it, I doubted myself and then I met some wonderful people in Maine who gave me a kick up the ass and told me to get writing. Thanks Pete, Amy and Katie. Thanks to you guys, it took me 10 days to do that final edit. The feeling of accomplishment and relief to have it all done is thanks to you.

Of course I have to thank the men along the journey. They shall remain nameless, but they know who they are. It may have looked different from your side, but this is my story and damn was it fun. Thank you.

Last but not least, thanks to my parents who were horrified to hear the genre of the novel, but nothing short of supportive in my endeavour to get my story out for those who were interested. It was a profound healing experience for me and I hope this brings them feelings of pride instead of shame (but please let this be the only section you read).

May this book give you the inspiration to explore your sexual freedom in whatever way that looks to you and never hold back.

www.ingramcontent.com/pod-product-compliance
Lightning Source LLC
Chambersburg PA
CBHW022002090426
42741CB00007B/863